A Theology of Preaching in the African-American Context

by

Dr. Clayton D. Furlow

Orman Press
Lithonia, Georgia

A Theology of Preaching in the African-American Context

Unless otherwise indicated, all scripture quotations are taken from the *Holy Bible, King James Version*.

Copyright © 2004
Dr. Clayton D. Furlow

Orman Press
4200 Sandy Lake Drive, Lithonia, GA 30038

ISBN: 1-891773-61-5

Printed in the United States of America

Dedication

This volume is dedicated to my loving wife, Marion, who encouraged me to have this work published; to my mother Gertrude Hester, who has been a source of inspiration and determination all of my life; to my children, Tony and Craig, whom I love dearly and who make me proud to be their father; to my daughters-in-law, Lea and Sonja, who have provided us with the daughters we never had; and finally, to the two little guys after my own heart, Cordell Alexander and Celia Renee, my grandchildren, who will read this book one day and, hopefully, will get a sense, of the kind of life I have tried to live before them.

Acknowledgements

I am greatly indebted to and would like to thank the following people for their invaluable assistance during the initial and final stages of this project:

Dr. William B. McClain, adjunct professor of homiletics at the Lutheran Theological Seminary at Philadelphia, for reviewing the proposal for my dissertation and providing invaluable suggestions.

Dr. Olin P Moyd, pastor of the Mount Lebanon Baptist Church, Baltimore, Maryland, who offered helpful suggestions regarding the content of the theological questionnaire.

Dr. Margaret A. Krych, associate dean for Graduate Education at the Lutheran Theological Seminary at Philadelphia, who was instrumental in editing this manuscript.

Dr. Katie Day, professor of church and society, for her suggestions during the writing process.

I would also like to thank the following pastors in the Philadelphia area for taking time out of their busy schedules to answer theological questions necessary for completing this project: Dr. William Banks, pastor emeritus, Faith Fellowship Baptist Church; Pastor Ralph Blanks of the Janes Memorial

United Methodist Church; Pastor Martha Lane of the Mt. Tabor A.M.E. Church; Dr. J. Wendell Mapson, pastor of the Monumental Baptist Church; Pastor Larry Marcus of the Greater Faith Baptist Church; Pastor James Moore Sr. of the Second Mt. Zion Baptist Church; Bishop Earnest Morris of the Mt. Airy Church of God and Christ; Pastor Emeritus Dr. Lee E. Peace (my mentor) of the Tabernacle West Baptist Church; Pastor Robert Shine of the Berachah Baptist Church; and to retired Pastor Frank Stevens of the Yeadon Presbyterian Church.

I am also indebted to members of the Baptist Pastors Conference of Philadelphia and Vicinity who provided helpful theological insights relative to the preaching task. I want to thank both my former pastor, the Reverend Arthur Lee Johnson, pastor emeritus of the St. Paul's Baptist Church, for his continued support throughout my seminary experience and the Reverend Dr. Lowell M. McCown, pastor of the McKinley Memorial Baptist Church, for the strong support he has given me since we became members of the McKinley family.

And last, but certainly not least, I wish to thank my wife, Marion, without whose computer skills and ability to edit the interviewing tapes, it would have been virtually impossible to complete this volume on time.

Table of Contents

Chapter 3: The Nature and Character of God in African-American Preaching

Chapter 4: Christology and Pneumatology in African-American Preaching

Conclusions

Appendices 137

Bibliography 209

Foreword

Given the plethora of needs that confront members of the African-American church, the preachers and pastor-theologians are constantly faced with critical theological questions that will inform what they say about the Christian faith. They must not only confront the critical life issues that confront their members, they must also give serious consideration to those doctrines of the church that inform the preaching task.

Historically, African-American preachers and pastor-theologians have not been preoccupied with systematic theological reflections in their sermon preparation and subsequently in their preaching. Traditionally, African American preachers and pastor-theologians have been more concerned with the life issues that are contained in the Bible than they have with addressing certain theological categories of the Christian faith. This does not mean that theology is not an integral part of African-American preaching; indeed, it is. What it means essentially is that practical theological applications have been and continue to be the natural extension of what African-American preachers and pastor-theologians include in the preaching process as they attempt to address the existential realities of the people whom they are called to serve. This however, has raised some very important questions with respect to theology and preaching: Is this rather indirect method of including theology in African-American preaching sufficient for the African-American church today, or is there a need for African-American preachers and pastor-theologians to be more theologically conscious in the preaching process? And if so, what should be the form and content of theological reflection in African-American preaching?

These are the questions that lead to a systematic study of the problem. This book documents the results of the study and the conclusions derived from its findings. My research included an investigation of the degree to which African-American history, context and hermeneutics inform modern day preaching. My desire is that the results of this study will motivate African-American preachers and pastor-theologians to look through some new and modified lenses of biblical interpretation to ensure their messages are existentially relevant to the needs of those who come to hear a word of hope each Sunday morning. Preachers and pastor-theologians must not only preach sermons about Jesus who transforms minds and souls, they must also preach about Jesus who liberates from social injustices. Perhaps, in these pages, you will find a greater understanding of the elements that influence the preaching task and inspiration to revise your theological language to meet the needs of today's African-American context.

Clayton D. Furlow

Introduction

The Issue in Context

From the antebellum period to the present, preaching has and continues to be the primary focus of worship in the African-American church. While the predominantly white Protestant mainline denominations such as Episcopalians and Lutherans have tended to be more liturgical in their worship experiences, the African-American church has characteristically relied upon the African-American preacher or the pastor-theologian to determine the style, mode, form, and content of worship. Indeed, the preacher or pastor is preeminent in the African-American church. He or she has often been called upon to be a politician, social activist, educator, and other such functions that his or her members may have needed.

In addition to the wide range of functions that the African-American preacher or pastor-theologian is called upon from time to time to perform, he or she is expected to bring a substantive word from the Lord that will address the people's fears, doubts, guilt, sins, and pessimistic outlook on life itself. Living in a world of secularism and relativism where the sin of greed and the struggle for power have affected an entire nation, members of the African-American church want to know if there is a word from the Lord in the present state of their afflictions. They want to know what in the world God is doing or what is God doing in the world on behalf of those who struggle from day to day with their backs against the wall of social injustices and marginalization. They also want to know if there is a word from the Lord for those who are trapped in the urban centers of our nation, where resources for education, housing, health care, and governmental services are constantly diminishing. And they also want to know if there is a word from the Lord in the midst of the unprecedented rise in unemployment among young African-American males, which is the antecedent to an illegal drug culture, crime, and homelessness.

These and other questions come before the preacher and pastor-theologian almost on a daily basis. They require the preacher or pastor-theologian to spend long hours in his or her study in prayer, devotion, and meditation, waiting sometimes with anxious anticipation for the Holy Spirit to speak to the pressing concerns of the people through the Scripture, *"what thus says the Lord."* The African-American preacher or pastor-theologian is not making inquiry regarding the ontological nature of God's being, nor is he or she concerned with the theoretical nature of God's transcendence. The preacher or pastor-theologian comes to the Scriptures in search of concrete answers to concrete problems.

Historically, the African-American preacher or pastor-theologian has and continues to face these problems with unrelenting zeal and spiritual compassion. He or she has looked and continues to look to the God of the Bible for new and renewed revelation that will give his or her people a sense of being in a social context of non-being. When those of the dominant culture have conspired to rob African Americans of their dignity and humanity, the preacher or pastor-theologian has constantly looked to the Bible for words of hope and transformation. When the distresses of racism dimmed the minds and spirits of their parishioners, insisting that they are not significant in the world, the African-American preacher or pastor-theologian has affirmed time and time again that God's word speaks to the contrary.

Clearly, the African-American preacher or pastor-theologian has been able to move into the thoughts and feelings of those whom he or she served, because traditionally, the preacher was in close contact with his or her parishioners. The African-American preachers were up to their ears and hearts with the conditions of the people, which would not have been possible if meaningful dialogue had not taken place. Because of the intimacy between the pastor and the people, the preacher or the pastor had a real sense of the social, political, educational, economic and spiritual issues that the members were facing on a daily basis.

The Problem

Given the plethora of needs that confront members of the African-American church, the preachers and pastor-theologians are constantly faced with critical theological questions that inform what they say about the Christian faith generally and about God in particular. They must not only confront the critical life issues that confront their members; they must also give serious consideration to those doctrines of the church that inform the preaching task. Olin Moyd rightly points out that preaching and theology are opposite sides of the same coin. "Preaching has been the primary vehicle for transmitting transcendent truths to the homes and hearts of the masses."[1]

Historically, African-American preachers and pastor-theologians have not been preoccupied with systematic theological reflections in their sermon preparations and subsequently in their preaching. Traditionally, African-American preachers and pastor-theologians have been more concerned with the life issues that are contained in the Bible than they have with addressing certain theological categories of the Christian faith. This does not mean that theology is not a part of African-American preaching; indeed it is. What it means essentially is that practical theological applications have been and continue to be the natural extensions of what African-American preachers and pastor-theologians include in the preaching process, as they attempt to address the existential realities of the people whom they are called to serve. This however, raises some very important questions with respect to theology and preaching: Is this rather indirect method of including theology in African-American preaching sufficient for our day in time, or do we need to be more theologically conscious in

---

1. Olin P. Moyd, *The Sacred Art: Preaching and Theology in the African-American Tradition*, (Valley Forge: Judson Press, 1995) 7.

the preaching process? And if so, what should be the form and content of theological reflection in African-American preaching?

Presupposition

It is this writer's belief that a theology of preaching is needed in African-American preaching in order to assist African-American preachers and pastor-theologians focus more systematically on those issues and problems that constantly confront their hearers. This is not to suggest that preachers and pastor-theologians should become preoccupied with preaching theology, rather, preaching should become the conscious effort through which the content of theology is delivered. If preaching is proclamation and theology is interpretation as Moyd insists, then the African-American preacher or pastor-theologian will need to be cognizant of both, if he or she is going to be both effective and affective in preaching sermons that are theologically sound and existentially relevant.

The content and form of theological reflection in African-American preaching must take seriously what African-American theologians and biblical scholars are saying regarding the Christian faith. They must give careful and thoughtful consideration to the cultural, historical, social, and religious context out of which the African-American preaching has emerged. Yet, African-American preaching must be careful that it does not become so one-dimensional in its theological interpretations that it fails to preach the whole counsel of God's plan. A theology of preaching in the African-American context must not only be concerned with the language and themes of black theology; it must also make use of some of the language from classical theology as well.

Review of Previous Research

Much has been written in the area of African-American preaching to date. Many African-American preachers and pastor-theologians have contributed greatly to the structural designs, styles, types, and methods that are included in African-American preaching and preparation. However, since this project is primarily concerned with those studies that are directly related to preaching and theology, the scope of this project will only allow for the inclusion of those studies that directly or indirectly apply to African-American preaching and theology.

In *The Sacred Art: Preaching and Theology in the African-American Tradition*,[2] Olin P. Moyd's book creates a synthesis between preaching and theology that has evolved into a creative and instructive system of proclamation and interpretation. He also shows how preaching and practical theology have been done by master African-American preachers and pastor-theologians. In a study on *Preaching Liberation*,[3] James H. Harris, analyzes the power of the gospel to speak to and transform individuals as well as the structures of society. He makes use of categories from black theology to discuss both sin and oppression in light of transformation and libera-

2. Ibid.
3. James H. Harris, *Preaching Liberation*, (Minneapolis: Fortress Press, 1995).

tion. Henry H. Mitchell's book on *Black Preaching: The Recovery of a Powerful Art*,[4] William B. McClain's *Come Sunday: The Liturgy of Zion*,[5] Gardner C. Taylor's *How Shall They Preach*,[6] Marvin A. McMickle's *Preaching to the Black Middle Class*,[7] Samuel D. Proctor's, *How Shall They Hear: Effective Preaching for Vital Faith*,[8] *A Certain Sound of the Trumpet: Crafting a Sermon of Authority*,[9] and H. Beecher Hicks', *Preaching Through a Storm*,[10] include theology as a necessary consideration in African preaching

While African-American theologians have been concerned primarily with systematic reflections on the Christian faith and its interpretations for the African-American community, their contributions to this study have been vitally important. Such studies include: James H. Evans, Jr.'s *We Have Been Believers: An African-American Systematic Theology*,[11] James H. Cone's *God of the Oppressed*,[12] *A Black Theology of Liberation:*

4. Henry H. Mitchell, *Black Preaching: The Recovery* , New York: Harper and Row Publishers, 1970, 1979.
5. William B. McClain, *Come Sunday: The Liturgy of Zion,* (Nashville: Abingdon Press, 1990).
6. Gardner C. Taylor, *How Shall They Preach*, (Elgin: Progressive Baptist Publishing House, 1977).
7. Marvin A. McMickle, *Preaching to the Black Middle Class*, (Valley Forge: Judson Press, 2000).
8. Samuel D. Proctor, *How Shall They Hear: Effective Preaching for Vital Faith,* (Valley Forge: Judson Press, 1992)
9. Samuel D. Proctor, *A Certain Sound of the Trumpet: Crafting a Sermon of Authority,* (Valley Forge: Judson Press, 1992).
10. Beecher H. Hicks, *Preaching Through a Storm*, (Grand Rapids.: Zondervan Publishing House, 1987).
11. James H. Evans, Jr., *We Have Been Believers: An African-American Systematic Theology*, (Minneapolis: Fortress Press, 1992).
12 James H. Cone, , *God of the Oppressed*, (Minneapolis: Seabury Press, 1975).

Twentieth Anniversary Edition,[13] J. Deotis Roberts' *Black Theology in Dialogue,*[14] *Africentric Christianity: A Theological Appraisal for Ministry,*[15] Olin P. Moyd's *Redemption in Black Theology,*[16] Cleophus J. LaRue's *The Heart of Black Preaching,*[17] Cain Hope Felder's (editor) *Stony The Road We Trod: African-American Biblical Interpretation,*[18] Dwight N. Hopkins' *Down, Up, and Over: Slave Religion and Black Theology,*[19] C. Eric Lincoln and Lawrence H. Mamiya's, *The Black Church in the African-American Experience*[20].

Method, Materials, and Source

The materials for this project have been gathered from four major sources: literary works on African-American religious history, preaching and theology, black theology, and interviews taken from African-American pastor theologians. The

13 James H. Cone, *A Black Theology of Liberation: Twentieth Anniversary Edition*, (Maryknoll, NY: Obis Books, 1990).

14. J. Deotis Roberts, *Black Theology in Dialogue*, (Philadelphia: The Westminster Press, 1987).

15. J. Deotis Roberts, *Africentric Christianity: A Theological Appraisal for Ministry*, (Valley Forge: Judson Press, 2000).

16. Olin P. Moyd, *Redemption in Black Theology,* (Valley Forge, PA.: Judson Press, 1979), 81.

17. Cleophus J. LaRue, *The Heart of Black Preaching*, (Louisville: Westminster John Knox Press, 2000).

18. Cain Hope Felder, editor, *Stony the Road We Trod: African-American Biblical Interpretation*, (Minneapolis: Fortress Press, 1991).

19. Dwight N. Hopkins, *Down, Up, and Over: Slave Religion and Black Theology*, (Minneapolis: Fortress Press, 2000).

20. C. Eric Lincoln and Lawrence H. Mamiya, *The Black Church in the African-American Experience*, (Durham and London: Duke University Press, 1990).

interviews were done with ten pastor-theologians in the Philadelphia area who represented various denominational traditions. Therefore, the conclusions reached will be limited to African-American pastor-theologians in Philadelphia and the immediate surrounding areas, although the findings may have wider geographical implications. The ten pastor-theologians interviewed were both males and females, from the Baptist, United Methodist Episcopal, African Methodist Episcopal, Presbyterian, and the Church of God in Christ denominations. These pastor-theologians were chosen because they represented both liberal and conservative views with respect to preaching and their interpretation of Scripture.

Each participant was asked to respond to various theological questions (see appendix) and how he or she interpreted each in his or her preaching. These responses in turn were tape recorded and subsequently transcribed so that they might be used in the theological categories in each chapter.

Chapter Divisions

The Introduction deals with the nature and context of the study and the method by which the problem will be addressed. Chapter 1 is concerned with African-American religious history. It focuses on those salient issues that have given rise to the African-American church's theology and preaching. Chapter 2 deals with the principles of African-American hermeneutics and what makes it unique for African-American preaching. Chapter 3 concentrates on the nature and character of God in African preaching. Chapter 4 deals with Christology and pneumatology as they relate to preaching in the African-American context. The Conclusion will summarize the project in order to arrive at a conclusion regarding the problem that was stated in the Introduction.

Chapter 1

History of African-American Thought

In order to understand and appreciate African-American preaching and the theology out of which it has emerged, one must of necessity understand and appreciate the historical context, which shapes its content. While this chapter on the history of African-American thought makes no attempt to be exhaustive (indeed it cannot), its primary aim is to list some of those salient issues and responses that have given rise to the African-American church's theology and preaching.

Slavery and Religion

When the Africans were captured and brought with force to America, they also brought with them a worldview, a belief system, and a theology. They brought with them a belief in a Supreme Being. W.E.B. Du Bois, an African-American scholar who wrote during the latter part of the nineteenth century and earlier part of the twentieth century, sees a kind of syncretism between the religious beliefs that the Africans brought to America and the Christianity which they subsequently embraced.

Du Bois interpreted the early African religion as being "nature-worship, with profound belief in invisible surrounding influences, good and bad, and his worship was through incantations and sacrifices."[21] Although these modes of worship and rituals were retained within the African and African-American culture and practices, they did undergo drastic revisions. The plantation organization replaced the clan tribe, and the white master replaced the chief with what was thought to be greater despotic powers. These radical changes in the social and religious life of the Africans and African Americans meant that the forced and long-continued toil became the rule of life.

> "The old ties of blood relationship and kinship disappeared and instead of the family, there appeared a new polygamy and polyandry, which in some cases almost reached promiscuity."[22]

The social fall-out of this kind of inhumane pressure, caused by the slave owners would mean the separation of the African and African-American family structure.

Yet, in spite of this social and religious revolution, Africans and African-Americans were able to retain some traces of the former group life. The primary remaining social artifact was the "Priest or Medicine-man."[23] He appeared early on the

---

21. W. E. B. Du Bois, *The Soul of Black Folks*, (Millwood: Krauss-Thompson Organizational Limited, 1973), 3.
22. Ibid., 195
23. Ibid.

plantation and functioned as a healer of the sick, the inter-preter of the Unknown, the comforter of the sorrowing, the supernatural avenger of the wrong, and the one who rudely but picturesquely expressed the longing, the disappointment, and the resentment of a stolen and an oppressed people. As one who shared the same kind of human-caused suffering and dehumanization as did his fellow African-American brothers and sisters, this tribal poet-singer, physician, judge, and priest, called upon all the resources of heathenism to assist him in overcoming this dark triumph of evil called slavery, which had come over him and his fellow African Americans.

Slavery was not only a time when African Americans experienced the triumph of evil over them; it was also a time when they believed that all the powers of the underworld were striving against them. The African-American chattel found himself living in a duality of existential absurdity. He was born with a veil and gifted with second sight in the American World, a world that yielded him no true self-consciousness, only let him see himself through the revelation of another world.

In spite of their desperate attempt to call upon witchcraft, the mysterious Obi worship with its barbarous rites, spells and blood sacrifices, the middle of the eighteenth century saw the African-American slave sink to a state of passive submission. Independent religious institutions were out of the question for the vast majority of African Americans, suffering the system of slavery in the southern states. They attended church, if they attended at all, with the whites or under white supervision. The new social political, economic, and religious systems of dehumanization and oppression made them the unwilling victims of a new philosophy of life, a doctrine of passive submission embodied in a newly learned Christianity.

The slave masters are said to have used this Christian propaganda to their advantage to indoctrinate African-American slaves with a different worldview. Courtesy became humility, moral strength degenerated into submission, and the exquisite native appreciation of the beautiful became an infinite capacity for dumb suffering. It appeared that the African slave was losing the joy of this world.

Yet, in the midst of dehumanization and oppression, the African-American slave began to look at the biblical text, not in the same manner in which he had been taught to believe, but in light of his own world and circumstances. Those who had learned to read, even if it were clumsily done, discovered a God who would be an avenging Spirit of the Lord enjoining patience in this world, under sorrow and tribulation until the Great Day when He would lead His children home. They found in the book of Exodus and in Psalm 68:31 the words of liberation and redemption. African Americans were empowered to overcome by hearing these words and interpreting them in light of their existential circumstances. Like the ancient Israelites, African Americans too, had been removed from their homeland by force; yet, they had survived, and had been empowered to overcome and to transcend the brutality of slavery and second-class citizenship because of divine intervention and divine help. Incidents of the stories of African-American survival, transcendence, and overcoming had been inextricably intertwined with Israel's stories of oppression and deliverance of the Old Testament and even the New Testament redemption stories. They tell of how Jesus of Nazareth came to "set the captives free and to bring them in to confederation where his kingdom would come on earth as it is in heaven."[24]

Subsequently, slaves developed their own "invisible institution."[25] In the slave quarters and brush arbors, they held their own religious meetings, where they interpreted their experiences by means of myths, stories, and symbols of Christianity. They were even willing to risk severe punishment to attend forbidden prayer meetings in order to worship God free of white control. They may not have fully understood all the implications of such a verse as Psalm 68:31. Yet, they continued to meditate upon it, linking the mythic present with the mythic past and future when *"princes shall come out of Egypt; Ethiopia and shall soon stretch out her hand to God" (Psalm 68:31)*. Indeed, African-American slaves believed that God would eventually stretch out His hands to the disinherited and underclass of society.

Unfortunately, African Americans soon learned that they were in for a rude awakening. The Civil War and emancipation seem to validate African-American identification with Israel, but African Americans discovered that racial oppression showed no signs of abating. Decades after emancipation, it seemed as though God had neither reached out His hands to redeem the black man, nor had the black man entered the Promised Land. The African Americans still faced disfranchise-

---

24. Moyd, *Redemption in Black Theology*, 81.
25. Ibid.

ment, lynching, and newly established codes of segregation in the nineteenth century, and African Americans were still left to struggle to understand what their destiny in America meant for them as a people.

Phases and Periods in African-American Religion

There have been various attempts to place the African-American religious struggle in a systematic order of progression. Dr. Olin P. Moyd does a critical analysis of a study conducted by Ruby F. Johnston who wrote *The Development of the Negro Religion*[26] in 1945. Dr. Moyd examines Johnston's three stages of religious development to which she refers as "shifts in Negro religion."[27] The first period is labeled "The Inception Stage."[28] She believes that this period extended from the beginning of African-American religion in America to the Civil War, and was marked by supernaturalism, simple rudiments of Christianity, and emotionalism. She believes the second phase of the first stage was marked by the rise of the Negro consciousness of race and efforts of the African-American leaders to secure freedom of worship and freedom to be persons. Emphasis and objectives were directed towards heaven. The second period in her analysis is called 'The Developmental Stage.'[29] She believes this stage began with the Emancipation Proclamation and extended to World War I

26. Moyd, *Redemption in Black Theology*, 62.
27. Ibid.
28. Ibid.
29. Ibid.

(from 1863 to about 1814). This stage of development was thought to be marked by a steady growth and development with emphasis shifting from civil and social right and active participation in government. While the heavenly elements were still central in African-American religion, it was thought to be somewhat diminished during this stage. Johnston called her third period "The Transitional Stage."[30] She believed this stage began in 1914 and continued to 1945. According to Johnston, this stage was characterized by tension arising as a result of both the decline and the struggle to return to emotionalism in African-American practice. She also saw a wane in traditional religious attitudes and a transferring of religion in this world. This, she contended, could be recognized in the political activities in the African-American churches, the social activities, with emphasis on recreation, and the African-American philosophies of American society as expressed in the church.

In Dr. Moyd's critique of Johnston's periods or stages of religious development, he determined that the primary emphases were preoccupied with the shifts of emotionalism in African-American religion. However, he failed to mention that she also emphasized that African-American leaders during those periods of religious development were similarly concerned with the freedom of worship and the freedom to be persons as opposed to non-persons in the ontological sense. Although Johnston's concentration on the shifts in emotionalism may have been helpful in tracing the shifts in emotional expression in African-American religion, Dr. Moyd

---

30. Ibid.

contends that it was inadequate for an understanding of the theology, which undergird any and all African-American religious expressions. Until recently, the problem with early research on African-American religious history has suffered perhaps from white stereotypes of African-American religion. As a result, most studies dealt—in large part—with whatever generally was considered to be the negative aspect of black religious history.

In Dr. Moyd's investigation of the development of African-American religion, he sees a vast contrast between what Johnston's investigation revealed and what has been the result of recent studies. While Dr. Moyd writes from a theological context, his findings can be easily applied to the present discussion of African-American religious development.

In Moyd's opinion, the development of African-American religion and theology covered a period of one hundred years, from the end of the Civil War to the present. Yet, he sees the mold of black theology and religion as being cast during the half century from the end of the Civil War to the beginning of the Great Migration, about 1914. He concluded in his investigation that African-American history could be divided into five periods, namely:

(1) **The Formative Period** from the end of the Civil War through the era of Reconstruction, 1877

(2) **The Maturation Period** after the era of Reconstruction to the beginning of the Great Migration, ca. 1914;

(3) **The Expansion-Renaissance Period** from the beginning of the Great Migration to the beginning of World War II

(4) **The Passive Protest Period**, World War II to 1955;

(5) **The Radical Reassertion Period** from 1955 to 1973.[31]

Dr. Moyd also points out that there was a formative period of about two hundred years of black presence in this land. This is also the period in African-American religious history, which Du Bois described as "the triumph of evil over the Negro."[32] Religiously, this might be referred to as the Transitive Period for African Americans. Definitely, it was not a time in history when the African slaves gave up their gods and religious beliefs and adopted those of the oppressors as has been erroneously taught and believed. In fact, the African scholar, Osadolor Imasogie is in disagreement with Du Bois who consigned African religion to that of heathism, witchcraft, and voodooism. Imasogie argues that such terms as *animism, fetishism, polytheism,* and *primitive monotheism* are inadequate as blanket terms in reference to African traditional religions.[33] In his analysis, and contrary to Western view, Africans believed in the embodiment of spirits in material objects, such as charms, amulets, and talishma. These objects served only as a subordinate part of the African religious complex. He argues that "all religions that uphold the doctrine of sacramen-

31. Ibid.

32. Du Bois, *The Soul of Black Folk*, 5.

33. Osadolor Imasogie, "African Traditional Religion and the Christian Faith," *Review and Expositor*, vol. 70, no. (summer, 1973), 283-293.

talism"[34] could logically be reduced to fetishism. It can also be logically argued that the African altars could very well function as aids in worship in the same way that the icon and the crucifix function in the Christian church.

Similarly, polytheism would have to be ruled out as an adequate term to refer to African religions since polytheism, in reference to Greek, Babylonian, and Egyptian gods meant gods of equal status, with no supreme God. This is not the case, Imasogie says in traditional African religion. He argues that whatever degree of difference there might be among African religious expression, "a belief in the Supreme Being remains the one golden thread running through the heart of their religious experience."[35] He quotes from John S. Mbiti in defining the African-American notion of God as the Supreme Being: "He is self-sufficient, self-supporting just as He is self-originating."[36] Moyd believes that *Bureaucratic Monotheism* is the term that best describes the African traditional religion for Imasogie, in that it reflects the sociopolitical pattern of African societies and the cultural patterns of the people that are also expressed in their religious practices. In their sociopolitical experiences, their day-to-day dealings were generally with the local chiefs and ministers, although the king had absolute power.

This new perspective challenged the old heathenistic and paganistic ideas of the religious views of the imported slaves supported by the thinking of such early scholars as Dubois.

34. Ibid.
35. Ibid.
36. Moyd, *Redemption in Black Theology*, 62–68.

Imasogie's findings make it clear that the slaves did not have to give up their bureaucratic monotheism views in order to accept the Christian religion, nor did they have to give up their concept of a Supreme Deity who, like their cultural tribal king, was generally inaccessible to the ordinary villagers and to the brush people. Imasogie believes that established religious doctrine of the slaves made it easy for them to accept Jesus Christ as an intermediary in the bureaucratic hierarchy, since they already possessed a bureaucratic hierarchical religious perspective into which he could be fitted.

Given the religious, cultural, and social contexts of slave religious history, Moyd argues that the induction of the African slaves into Christianity was more a matter of religious transition and modification than it was a matter of a complete break with something old and useless and the acceptance of a religious psychic that was completely new and useful. In this process of religious transition and modification, the slaves retained much of their African modes of expressions. However, these modes of religious expressions were never appreciated or adopted by white Christians in America.

A further investigation of Moyd's Transitional or Formative period reveals that African slaves had little opportunity to continue to practice their own religion except through the invisible church of their own making. However, in South America, according to Moyd, slaves were grouped in large masses and were permitted to retain their drums and much of their material culture. This was not the case in North America. Slaves who spoke the same dialects were usually separated, and their drums and percussion instruments were denied.

Ortiz Walton tells of how slaves in Trinidad, Haiti, and Jamaica were permitted to retain their percussion instruments and their African music orientation, but the enforcement of anti-drum laws in the United States made it necessary to transfer the function of the drum to the feet, hands, and body by way of the spirituals during the slave era.

Dr. Moyd also notes that it was during the Transitional or Formative period that the African-American church, as it were, began to assert its own understanding of the Christian faith—its own theology. Although theological reflection had not been put down in writing, it could be heard in the oral tradition in many black churches on a Sunday morning. It might be heard in the form of a song: "It is no secret what God can do, for what He has done for others He will do for you," meaning what God did in delivering the biblical characters from their earthy woes, He would also do for those who are inflicted with earthy woes today. Or it may have come in the form of a prayer: "Lord, I know that you are still pulling down mountains and elevating valleys." Moyd contends that this redemptive understanding of the Christian faith was well formulated by the end of the Reconstruction era.

> The historical incidents of widespread oppression and segregation following the era of Reconstruction provided the necessity for the maturation of African-American theology in the succeeding periods.[37]

---

37. Ibid.

While the African-American church was in the process of formulating its own theology and practice, Rutherford B. Hayes was aspiring to become president of the United States in 1876. It was during this period that African Americans suffered their most drastic setbacks, says Moyd.

> After the election of Hayes, the state legislatures in every state of the Union passed laws stripping African Americans of rights they had gained through the era of Reconstruction. The Supreme Court struck down Civil Rights Acts. Jim Crow laws went into effect in many states. Federal troops were withdrawn from the South. The abolitionists lost interest in and/or effectiveness with African Americans in the South. By the end of the century, African-American politicians were virtually weeded out through various and devious means. The problems of African Americans during this period were further intensified.[38]

By the end of the century, measures were taken to make sure that no blacks were elected again. "It was more than half a century, in 1963 before another black person was elected in Georgia."[39] "Disfranchisement was effectuated through such measures as poll taxes, literary tests, previous voting records, grandfather clauses, and knowledge of the Constitution."[40] In

38. Ibid.
39. Ibid.
40. Ibid.

addition, the Supreme Court in 1896 set a pattern for legal separation of the races for the next half century with its separate but equal decree. But in spite of these horrific setbacks, the African-American preachers and pastor-theologians went about the task of refining their understanding of Scripture and doctrine, and their understanding of how God was revealing Himself in the world—especially through a dehumanized black people.

The Emergence of the Preacher-Pastor-Theologian

Yet, it is out of this other world, this duality of existence, this existential absurdity that a syncretism between Christianity and African religion emerged. It is also within this historical and religious context that we see the emergence of the African-American preacher. Du Bois refers to him as the most unique personality developed by the Negro on American soil. One can easily understand the uniqueness of the African-American preacher when one considers that he is first of all a spiritual leader. Yet, he can be perceived as a politician, a boss, an intriguer, and an idealist. "The combination of a certain resourcefulness with deep-seated earnestness, with consummate ability, gives him his preeminence and helps him maintain it."[41]

Using their God-given ability and their influence, pastor-theologians, such as, Absalom Jones, William Miller, George Washington Williams, Alexander Crummell, John Jasper,

41. Du Bois, *The Soul of Black Folk,* 191.

Francis Grimke and many others, attempted to put the African-American struggle in theological perspective. As early as 1808, Absalom Jones, pastor of St. Thomas African Episcopal Church in Philadelphia questioned the theodicy of God. In his sermons, he wrestled with how the reality of a faithful, loving, compassionate, and just God would permit such a dehumanizing atrocity such as slavery. To him this was a great mystery. "Why would the imperial Father of the human race permit the transportation of so many of our fellow creatures to this country, to endure all the miseries of slavery?[42] One could conjecture that it may have been God's design, that in the midst of this dark period, the African-American slave would gain knowledge of the gospel, and would subsequently be qualified to be messengers of it to the land of their fathers. Jones' response was not so much an answer to this disturbing question as it was an admission that neither he, nor any person did really know for certain God's will. Jones, along with other ministers knew that the evangelization and civilization of the African-American slaves was the rationale used by Europeans, from the mid fifteenth century on to justify enslaving Africans. In Robateau's estimation, this ideology came dangerously close to absolving whites of their guilt for slavery. Nevertheless, ministers and pastor-theologians refused absolution by distinguishing God's will from His permission. In other words, God wills good. He only permits evil, and from it draws good. Although "God permitted these things to come to pass," William Miller preached, "It does not follow that the oppressors of Africa were not culpable for their

---

42. Robateau, *Fire in the Bones*, 24.

savage treatment to the unoffending African."[43] George Washington Williams echoed similar sentiments two generations later:

> God often permits evil on the ground of man's free agency, but He does not commit evil. The Negro of this country can turn to his Saxon brothers and say, 'As for you, ye meant it unto evil, but God meant it unto good; that we, after learning of your arts and sciences might return to Egypt and deliver the rest of our brethren who are yet in the house of bondage.'[44]

In addition to Jones, Miller, and Williams, Grimke too, was faced with the same theological problem as generations of African-American pastors before him. He too sought to find some meaning, some message of hope in the midst of so much suffering and despair. Grimke was convinced that things could not go on as they were at the present time. He did not place his hope or the hope of his suffering African-American brothers and sisters on political parties or government, but on the faith in the power of the religion of Jesus Christ. Grimke saw the purpose and providence of God from a Christological perspective where the teaching and preaching of Jesus Christ would break down the wall of separation, and would weld together men of all races in one great brotherhood.

---

43. Ibid., 46.
44. Ibid.

In sermonic style and prophetic form, hope and alienation interacted with each other with every word Grimke spoke. The profound depth and magnitude of his thoughts and reflections can be felt from a portion of one of his sermons:

> In spite of the shallowness and emptiness and glaring hypocrisy of the church, I still believe that Christianity is in the land. Today, it is like a little grain of mustard seed, but it has entered the soil, germinated and is springing up. It is like a little lump of leavens, which the woman hid in three measures of meal: but it has begun to work, and will continue to work, diffusing itself until the whole is leavened. God has promised to give to His Son the heathen for His inheritance and the uttermost parts of the earth for His possession: and in that promise this land is included. Christianity shall one day have sway even in the Negro-hating America; the spirit, which it inculcates, is sure, sooner or later, to prevail. I have myself, here and there, seen its transforming power. I have seen white men and women under its regenerating influence lose entirely the caste feeling. Jesus is yet to reign in this land. I will not see it, you will not see it, but it is coming all the same. In the growth of Christianity, true, real, genuine Christianity in

this land, I see the promise of better things for us as a race.[45]

We can only guess what these profound words of hope meant for those black souls who were being brutalized and lynched on a regular basis. Although these promises may have had a divinely appointed destiny, their fulfillment seemed to lie in some distant and remote future. Pastors, as well as lay persons continued to struggle with this quandary in sermons, speeches, tracts, convention minutes, history books resolutions, and editorials, from the beginning of the nineteenth century to the end. They searched the Bible, hoping to find in God's Word, signs of His will for the African-American race.

Yet, it was out of these struggles and experiences that African-American pastor-theologians began to reflect theologically on what God was doing in the world. Robateau's studies point out that African Americans fashioned a theology of history whose conclusion were these:

> Those who oppress and enslave others, those who make war, those who spread "civilization" by conquest, those who degrade other races, those who corrupt Christianity by making it a clan religion are destined to destroy one another. Their age will shortly end. A new age will shortly begin. In this new age, it will be the destiny of those who were enslaved but did not

---

45. Ibid., 40.

enslave, those who were hated but did not hate, to realize the gospel of the earth.[46]

Black Religion and Black Protest

In addition to theological reflections on the struggles confronting African Americans in the nineteenth century, African-American protest was also on the rise. Roboteau observed that protest in the nineteenth century had been predominantly religious, and that many of the leaders were ministers. The churches served as major forums for organizing and expressing black grievances, and the primary symbols of protest were religious ones. However, the first decade of the twentieth century witnessed the emergence of such organizations as the National Association for the Advancement of Colored People (NAACP) and Marcus Gravey's Universal Negro Improvement Association (UNIA). Though some scholars contend that African-American protest became more secularized during this time, Roboteau argues that the black church remained more political and more religious than some may have thought. Although such secular organizations as the NAACP and the UNIA were not directly attached to the church, they justified their goals by appealing to religious ideals. The NAACP, for example, attempted to get the republic to practice its faith by using the guardians of faith, the court system.

---

46. Ibid., 62.

On the other hand, Marcus Garvey, who is thought to have been the architect of the largest mass movement African Americans had ever seen, established his organization on the principles of the brotherhood of man and the fatherhood of God. Garvey's method and plan called for the syncretizing of democracy and Christianity. In his program and practice, the major thrust was an attempt to embody in an African republic, a black nation destined to unite the scattered children of Africa around the world. Though many people criticized Garvey with being anti-white, he denied their criticism by pointing out the despair of the African-American people of not achieving justice in this country. Yet, in his effort to gather black Americans and transpose them to their Republic of Africa, he also inspired civic piety among African-American masses and structured their piety around symbols appropriate for an African-American civil religion. Roboteau observed that the Universal Negro Improvement Association offered African Americans a cultural nationalism of their own, freed of ambivalence and alienation. To this end, Garvey's movement developed its own hymnal, creed, catechism, and baptismal ritual.[47]

Marcus Garvey was just one of the major players in the African-American religious protest in the early part of the twentieth century. There were those also who began to formulate for themselves an entirely new "religioracial" identity divorced of American thinking. The dichotomy between what true Christianity stood for and the travesty of white Christian

47. Ibid., 65.

doctrine and behavior as it applied to African Americans became unacceptable for some. According to Robateau:

> They found it virtually impossible, in light of white Christians' racism, to distinguish between true and false Christianity and condemned the entire religion as white man's propaganda.[48]

For them, the tension involved in holding the same religion as the oppressor proved too great. Psychologically, they felt that Christianity was for the white people. As Roboteau points out, it was at this time when we began to witness esoteric versions of Judaism and Islam staking their claims for African Americans' allegiance. An uncompromising spirit fostered by white Christian hypocrisy led some to abandon America and embrace an alienation that had been forced upon them. African Americans began to search for citizenship and acceptance in such a world as the Nation of Islam, under the leadership of Elijah Muhammed and Malcolm X, who preached a message of a "satanic" America.

As African-American protest continued into the twentieth century, a reflection on its previous history has revealed that it has not been as secular, nor has the African-American church been silent in protest, as some have argued. Roboteau reminds us that African-American pastor-theologians played an active role in the Garvey movement, the NAACP, and in local political affairs, both in the North and in the South. Robateau wrote:

---

48. Ibid.

But compared to the kind of religious protest that took place in the 1960's, clergy involvement in the early part of the twentieth century may not have been so radical.[49]

However, such pastors as Martin Luther King Sr. led several thousand demonstrators on a march from Ebenzer Baptist Church to City Hall in Atlanta in support of voting rights in 1935. The Reverend Adam Williams, the maternal grandfather of Dr. Martin Luther King Jr., is said to have organized rallies at Ebenezer to protest a municipal bond issue that contained no provisions for high school education for African-American youth.

It is probably safe to say that the activism of the pastor-theologians in the early part of the twentieth century laid the groundwork for the movement that began in Montgomery where African-American religious protest took on national and international significance.[50]

Therefore, when Dr. Martin Luther King Jr. came upon the national scene, he came with a rich history and tradition of social activism. As the son, grandson, and great-grandson of Baptist pastors who had been involved in religious protest, he too found himself following in this tradition. Like so many of

49. Ibid., 91.
50. Ibid.
53. Ibid.

the other protest movements, the nonviolent movement had its origin in the church. Although the social implications of the nonviolent movement dealt with the material concerns of the African-American people, the context was profoundly religious. Yet, for King, social justice and religion seemed inseparable. Many whites and some African Americans felt that civil rights were really a political rather than religious issue. In their opinion, Christian ethics were personal, not social. But for those who heard King's sermons and speeches, it was clear that both theology and Scripture went hand and hand when he addressed the social injustices faced by Africans Americans. Kings' ability to apply theology, ethics, and Scripture to the social blight surrounding him enabled him to hammer out for himself, and for the public (hostile and friendly) a nonviolent movement of black protest. As Robateau said, "At the core of King's protest was the principle of the non-cooperation with evil."[51]

Dr. King was able to show the relationship of suffering, with all its associations to the slaves past. "King's doctrine of redemptive suffering enabled him to reflect upon the old themes within African-American religious culture."[52] His prayers, sermons, and the traditional songs echoed black suffering of the past. He reflected upon freedom as God's promise of liberation for a dehumanized people, often quoting passages and verses from the Bible that triggered both memories and emotions. "And his letters from a Birmingham's jail

51. Ibid., 65–70.
52. Ibid.

connected the Christian movement with that of early Christian movement of Paul's day.[53]

In spite of all the progress made by King and the nonviolent movement, there were some black activists who were disappointed with the slow pace of racial change and disillusioned with the nonviolent movement. In 1966, the cry of black power became the rallying cry for those who adopted a more radical position than that of King's. As King refused to acquiesce to the more radical position of the black power adherents, other cult groups such as the Nation of Islam, with such notables as Malcolm X, preached a doctrine of liberation "by whatever means necessary." The assassination of King in 1968 led to massive rioting in urban areas around the country and seemed to confirm that the period of nonviolent religious protest had come to an end. Instead of attempting to achieve social justice through nonviolent passive resistance, the black Muslims and other radical groups sought to acquire self-determination, community control, and liberation by taking a more militant stand. Black pride and celebration of black cultural identity marked the new mood of independence among African Americans. Desegregation and integration were no longer used as catchwords to describe the black power movement. "Radical militants joined the black Muslims in attacking the African-American church for being otherworldly, compensatory, and reactionary."[54]

Chapter 2 will deal with African-American theological hermeneutics and its implications for the preaching task.

---

53. Ibid.
54. Ibid.

Chapter 2

African-American Theological Hermeneutics and Preaching

Aim and Definition

This chapter will deal with those hermeneutical principles that inform African-American preaching. The sociocultural and historical contexts determine how the preacher-pastor-theologian interprets the Scripture in ways that come alive and are made meaningful for those who seek to hear a substantive word from the Lord each Sunday morning. It is a word that is derived out of African Americans' unique understanding of God's activities in the midst of their existential realities. Those African-American pastor-theologians who mount the pulpit each Sunday morning may be in danger of doing great damage to the integrity of good black preaching if they adhere rigidly to some sterile, all-purpose homiletic, devoid of any reference to or knowledge of the sociocultural experiences of African Americans.

Harvey defines *hermeneutics,* in the broad universal sense, as:

That inquiry concerned with the presuppositions and rules of the interpretation of some form of human expression, usually a written text, although it can also be an artistic expression of some kind.[55]

In the Greek language, the verb simply means to interpret, to explain, and in the passive voice, it points to the meaning of something or to something that is translated. While this definition may be applied to essentially any text or expression, African-American theological hermeneutics is primarily preoccupied with the task of trying to understand what in the world God was and is doing on the behalf of black folks whose backs are constantly against the wall, and who live lives of existential contradictions.

In order for the pastor-theologian to preach sermons that are both affective and effective, she or he must come to grips with both the sociocultural and the historical implications of biblical interpretation. The preacher-pastor-theologian who dares to enter the sacred world of biblical interpretation must also risk being changed him or herself. Tisdale argues that one does not dance very closely with Scripture under the ongoing inspiration of God's Spirit without being addressed—and potentially transformed—by the encounter.[56] The same can be said for the pastor-theologian who is constantly and conscien-

55. Van A. Harvey, *A Handbook of Theological terms* (New York: Collier Books MacMillan Publishing Co., 1964), 117.
56. Leonora Tubbs Tisdale, *Preaching as Local Theology and Folk Art* (Minneapolis: Fortress Press. 1997), 93.

tiously attending to the struggles, fears, joys, and hearts of a congregation. They too will be changed in some way by the encounter.

This represents no new revelation for African-American pastor-theologians, for their lives have been and continue to be inextricably tied to the lives of those whom they have endeavored to serve since their antebellum days and chattel existence. In other words, the African-American pastor-theologian must not only have a working knowledge of the theoretical and abstract descriptions of biblical interpretation; he or she must also be cognizant of a new kind of hermeneutics as it is applied to the African-American tradition.

Neither the Greek term nor the German term is able to legitimatize the culture out of which the African-American experiences emerge. Pastor-theologians who wish to be theologically relevant in today's preaching must understand the folk-patterns of interpretation. This is not to suggest that the black preacher should sacrifice academic training and preparation for the sake of being "black." Nor does it mean that the black preacher must trade learned language for a more indigenous vocabulary. The African-American pastor-theologian has the responsibility to be both academically prepared and theologically relevant. In other words, he or she must be able to make the gospel plain.

Mitchell, quoting from Gerhard Ebeling's *Word and Faith*, states that the Word of God must be left to assert itself in an unflinchingly critical manner against distortions and fixations. But...theology and preaching should be free to make translation into whatever language is required at the moment and to refuse to be satisfied with correct archaizing repetition of pure doctrine.[57]

Although scholars of the Western world have influenced African-American hermeneutics to some degree, this fact has not sacrificed orthodoxy for orthopraxis. Black theologians have and continue to borrow from existing Western vocabulary, yet, there is a distinct difference between the way the white church reflects upon the Christian faith and the way African Americans reflect upon the Christian faith. The fact that black and white churches are not usually in constant contact with each other may be partly responsible for the differences. The other reason for this difference, and the one that makes more sense, is the difference in cultural and sociocultural contexts. Unscathed by proud abstractions of the Western world, African Americans read and listened to the Scripture and told the story in the manner of their own African heritage. Just as Martin Luther and the Reformation created a hermeneutic for the descendants that would follow, African-American hermeneutics also looked into the message and tradition of the past in order to see what African-American ancestors might be saying to black people today.

One of the vital lessons to be learned from a history of tradition in African-American biblical interpretation is that whatever particular genre was chosen, whether narrative or some other form, preachers and pastor-theologians never told those stories for the sake of mere entertainment. While the white culture may have been preoccupied with other prob-

---

57. Henry H. Mitchell, *Black Preaching: The Recovery of a Powerful Art* (Nashville: Abingdon Press, 1990), 18.

lems, African-American preachers and pastor-theologians were always concerned with survival and their ability to hold on until they received some relief from their present situation. No matter how charming or captivating the form and oratory style of the preacher may have been, the black preacher was about the serious business of leading people to grow in some spiritual or moral way by focusing on problems that confronted people on a daily basis. The being and kingdom of God were not preached in some abstract or esoteric language that had no meaning for a life of struggle. Rather, God, His being, and His kingdom were presented in the existential realities of the here and now. Preachers and pastor-theologians knew that people who were constantly being oppressed by systemic social injustice needed to hear those gut-survival themes that would provide nourishing certainty in difficult times. "Be as learned as you like," they seem to say, "but talk about something we can enter into, and give us something practical and certain."[58]

Even though the African-American ancestors did not know anything about Heideggers' linguistic existentialism, black preachers and pastors preached from combined memory and narrative interpretation in the common tongue with freshness and relevancy. They declared the gospel in the language and culture of the people. Since they were deprived of schooling for the most part, these pastor-theologians were limited to their own culture. Thus, they were forced to elaborate on the biblical stories with imagination. By doing so, the African-

58. Ibid., 105.

American preacher-theologian was able to make the gospel come alive for those who made their way to the churches Sunday after Sunday, because he spoke to their current needs.

History of Interpretation

Just as it is imperative for the African-American pastor-theologian to have an understanding of African-American history, it is equally imperative that she or he understands the styles, methods, and motives that informed earlier preaching. Indeed, these early pastor-theologians have passed on a tradition of biblical interpretation that is invaluable for those who dare to understand and preach the gospel of Jesus Christ to those who are victims of social injustice, racial discrimination, caste, and all the other social maladies that rob them of their true being. The pastor-theologian who preaches to the struggles and suffering of an oppressed, marginalized people must be willing to hear the voices of those from the ancient past as well as those of the eighteenth and nineteenth centuries. The voices of the ancient prophets, such as Amos, Jeremiah, Isaiah, and Daniel should be prerequisite for an understanding of how God acted on behalf of the underclass of society. Not only should these ancient prophets of the past be read, we should also hear the voices of such notables as Sojourner Truth, David Walker, John Brown, Harriet Tubman, William Miles, Richard Allen, James Verick, Daniel Alexander Payne, James W.C. Pennington, Henry Highland Garnet, Samuel Ringgold Ward, Alexander Crummel, Edwards Parks, Martin

Luther King, Jr., and countless others, less known but yet of great significance.

The Biblical Text

These pioneers of the African-American struggle in America brought new meanings and insights to the Bible. Just as white preachers tended to interpret the biblical events more theoretically, African-American pastor-theologians tended to interpret them more literally and concretely. They read and interpreted the Scripture in light of their own existential realities. The Bible came alive for them as they identified their own oppression with the historical characters of the ancient text. These earlier preachers, pastor-theologians, and social activists understood that the events of the Bible spoke powerfully and directly to their situations.

For example, the book of Genesis was not seen merely as a historical recapitulation of how and what God did in the creation of the world. African-American preachers and pastor-theologians saw in such stories as Jacob and Esau, and Joseph and his brothers how God could take potentially destructive and oppressive situations and turn them into something redeeming and liberating. From its very early inception, members of the African-American church have believed and continue to believe that God is not only the creator of the universe, but that He is also the supreme heavenly Father who establishes confederation among the human community. These and other Genesis stories have removed to a large degree the usual stereotypical literal interpretation found in the Genesis narratives. In some ways, these presuppositions have helped to extricate the stories from their racist entanglements where the Bible and the Christian faith are concerned. Long before the "New Hermeneutics," African-American preachers and pastor-theologians discovered a perspective of humanity that was completely different from that which they experienced in the teaching and practices of white Americans. Whatever the African-American preacher-pastor-theologian lacked in scholarship, he made up for with a keen sense of dedication and vivid imagination. In a sense, he created a new paradigm, indeed, a new "Black Hermeneutics" for biblical interpretation.

These African-American preachers and pastor-theologians learned early on from their white evangelical contemporaries that one's faith was not only derived from reading and studying the Bible, but that one was allowed to interpret the Bible freely. African Americans realized too that they could also interpret the Bible in light of their sociocultural and sociopolitical contexts. Just as white evangelicals could read some things and ignore others, so could African Americans. However, there is a danger in this kind of hermeneutical discrimination. There is the danger, as Tisdale argues, that such an interpretative method "may simply reinforce local world views and values, rather than challenging and stretching them."[59] Tisdale is correct in her observations; yet, it must be remembered that African Americans had to make a choice between a God who supported slavery and dehumanization

---

59. Tisdale, *Preaching as Local Theology and Folk Art*, 86.

and a God who stands on the side of the oppressed. For African Americans then and now, the choice is without contemplation. Indeed, the God of the Bible came to represent a virtual language world that African Americans could enter, and to some degree manipulate in light of their social experiences. After all, that which was of the Spirit or not of the Spirit had to be interpreted by the Spirit Himself.

It was the Holy Spirit who interpreted the Scriptures for a people who needed words of hope in a time of severe persecution and dehumanization. It was the Holy Spirit who led these early African-American pioneers of the Christian faith to the narratives of the Hebrew Bible. They were able to make similar comparisons to the Hebrews' bondage and escape and the oracles of the eight-century prophets' denunciations of social injustice. Under the unction of the Holy Spirit, these African-American preachers and pastor-theologians could envision a world where social justice would one day become a reality. They were able to look to the passion and resurrection of Jesus Christ, along with other New and Old Testament texts as the emergence of a new "canon."

Their faith was not one seeking understanding in a metaphysical sense, rather it was identified with the heroes and heroines in the Hebrew Bible and with the long-suffering, but ultimately victorious Jesus. It was seen in their sermons, songs, prayers, testimonies, and addresses. Just as God delivered the people of the Hebrew Bible from enslavement, the African-American could also sing without reservation that they too would be delivered. Just as Jesus suffered unjustly but was raised from the dead to new life, they understood that they would be "raised" from their "social death" to new life.

Long before African-American preachers and pastors knew about or were even allowed to attend theological institutions, they were interpreting the Bible in terms of their existential realities. It was the preachers and pastors who interpreted the Scripture historically and concretely. They are the ones who told the stories of Israel liberated from the bondage of Egypt; of the three Hebrew boys in the fiery furnace; of the dry bones in the valley; and the birth, suffering, sorrow, death, burial, and resurrection of Jesus Christ.

As a result of their preaching and their interpretation of the Scripture, thousands upon thousands of African Americans embraced the Christian faith after hearing not only the good news of God's promise of salvation sin and death, but also what God had done for the oppressed in biblical times. African-American preachers and pastors understood God as identifying with their struggles and the struggles of their people in a literal manner. Thus, as these biblical stories were told and retold, heard and reheard, they inculcated a preeminence of perseverance, strength, and hope in hopeless situations and circumstances. They provided hope for those who identified with the freed Israelites, the rescued Hebrew boys, the life-giving spirit of the dry bones in the valley, and the hope of the resurrection as experienced in the conquering of the grave by Jesus Christ. Those passages of Scripture that were unclear, or seemed to show God tolerating oppression, or not acting in a consistent fashion to obliterate some form of social blight upon marginalized people were seldom preached. LaRue explains:

> Recalcitrant Egyptian Pharaohs in the Old Testament, the Onesimus slave story in the New Testament, as well as other Pauline passages were declared in many instances to be inconsistent with the overall intention and action of God.[60]

Just as white pastor-theologians have interpreted the Scriptures in light of the status quo, African-American pastor-theologians interpreted Scripture in light of systemic and capricious discrimination confronting them. Jesus was seen as being a friend to the downtrodden and the outcast. African-American pastor-theologians were not preoccupied with trying to locate the historical Jesus in a theoretical and an abstract sense; they were more concerned with "What a Friend we have in Jesus." For African Americans, Jesus is not only divine; he is also human and identifies with the poor by suffering on their behalf. He is the same Jesus who is the risen Christ and the soon coming judge. This Jesus is in solidarity with those seeking to eradicate injustices and give courage and motivation to those who are sustained by his grace.

Therefore, according to LaRue, when African-American preachers and pastor-theologians came to the preparation of

---

60. Cleophus J. LaRue, *The Heart of Black Preaching* (Louisville: Westminster John Knox Press, 2000),. 15.

their sermons, there were at least two critical questions they wanted to address:

> How do I demonstrate to God's people through the proclamation of the Word the mighty and gracious acts of God on their behalf, and how best shall I join together Scripture and their life situation in order to address their plight in a meaningful and practical manner?[61]

LaRue argues that the first question is initiated by searching the Scriptures in order to find that portion that will conform to the "template" out of their sacred story. The second question is designed to help the preacher focus on a particular aspect of black experience.

These questions also require the preacher and pastor-theologian to make a meaningful connection between an all-powerful God and a marginalized, powerless people. A careful analysis of the biblical text enables the preacher and pastor-theologian to explicate those selected passages of Scripture. It is first and foremost the biblical text that will be the ground and starting point for any analysis of interpretation. Whatever is said about God and God's relationship to a marginalized people must possess Scriptural integrity. African-American preaching has been and continues to be shaped by this fundamental aim. This distinctiveness in African-American preaching is what LaRue refers to as the "template" through which Africans view Scripture and from which the end result

---

61. Ibid., 19.

can accurately be described as a "black sermon." It may be, as Mitchell suggests, that "this way of preaching in Black is quite possibly the best example extant of the new approach to interpretation."[62]

Context and Method

African-American preaching is contextual preaching. It is what Tisdale refers to as:

> The interpretation of the of the paradigmatic vision of God, humanity, and the world given in Scripture in a manner that is both faithful (in its whole and parts) and also capable of capturing and transforming the imagination of a particular congregation of hearers.[63]

Contextual preaching in Tisdale's description is not unique to African-American preaching. For the African-American preacher and pastor-theologian have always utilized the Scriptures when it came to capturing and transforming the lives of its hearers. Yet, when preaching is viewed as local theology, Scripture is not interpreted in isolation, but in dialogue and tension with the experience and perspectives of a local community of faith.

These experiences become even more meaningful when the African-American preacher and pastor-theologian reflect

---

62. Mitchell, *Black Preaching*, 18.
63. Tisdale, *Preaching as Local Theology and Art*, 95–96.

upon the sordid and painful memories of stories passed on from one generation to the next. It is through these stories, written and spoken, that we come to a better understanding of the meaning of life for those who exist on the fringes of society—the minorities, the poor, the weak, and the powerless.

Thus, contextual preaching for the African-American pastor-theologian requires that she or he be willing to unload much of the traditional theological baggage that has been dominated by Western thinking. The African-American pastor-theologian must be willing to reinterpret, revise, and undo much of what has been spoken and written by white theologians. African-American pastor-theologians must come to realize that no theology of preaching is universal and normative for all time and conditions. A theology of preaching is contextual theology. It means that she or he must go back and delve into the pages of history in order to get a better understanding of the religion of the slave foreparents and their experience of God and the power of the Holy Spirit. It is only through this "circling back" that the African-American pastor-theologian acquires an understanding of the religion and culture as a dynamic interaction between past and present. It is through this circling back that we get a feel for the horror and agony, pain and suffering, joy and sorrow, despair, and hope of those who journeyed on the slave ships to the shores of antebellum America. Circling back may be used also as a metaphor for a "circle of culture" since it identifies the experiences of a particular people. According to Harris, this circle of culture:

Enables the black preacher to interpret the gospel and the current social situation in a way that speaks to the hurts and fears as well as the hopes and dreams of oppressed people in our particular community and throughout the world.[64]

Concomitant with the idea of circling back or circle of culture is what Justo Gonzalez and Catherine Gonzalez have to say in reference to liberation theology:

To be able to do liberation theology, a person must first have gone through the painful experience of this circleeration theology which is grounded on a basic suspicion.[65]

It is a suspicion that compels the African-American preacher and pastor-theologian to examine with critical integrity the theology and history traditionally written about God and His revelation in the world in general, and black folk in particular. For the preacher and pastor-theologian who take contextual preaching and theology seriously, the exegetical process cannot be left totally in the hands of the academic community. This is not to say that the biblical scholars of the academy are incapable of responsible theological reflection. The problem is that most of these scholars' theology is

---

64. James H. Harris, *Liberation Preaching* (Minneapolis: Fortress Press, 1995), 61.
65. Ibid, 62.

produced out of a Western context and has little, if any, experience with the African-American struggle. Either explicitly or implicitly, Euro-centric traditions and the status quo of the dominant culture tend to slant their exegesis and theological reflections. This means that we need more African-American scholars pursuing such areas as theology and Biblical studies. We also need African-American preachers and pastor-theologians to view commentaries and other preaching aids with greater suspicion and critical open-mindedness, and to preach from the contextual experiences of the underclass.

This also means that contextual preaching and theology are practical enterprises. That is, they take into consideration the setting in which worship takes place. They also take into account the scriptural beliefs, history, experiences, culture, revelation, reason, and tradition of the preacher and the hearer. Contextual preaching and theology are multidimensional in the sense that both contextual theology and preaching include the spatial and the universal, the concrete and the abstract, the tangible and the intangible.

Indeed, theology and preaching take place in each of these contexts. Whereas, Dr. Olin Moyd prefers to list them separately, they can be grouped into two distinct categories, the physical and the psychological. The physical contexts would include the concrete, the tangible, and the spatial. On the other hand, the psychological contexts would include the universal, the abstract, and the intangible. Dr. Moyd is correct in concluding that the physical context for preaching takes place within the worship centers or churches and the places of social gathering, but it is the preaching, under the unction of the Holy Spirit that engenders responses of aspiration and celebration for a pilgrim people in the struggle for redemption and liberation. It is when the Holy Spirit speaks through the socio-religious experiences of those who worship that life is affirmed in the midst of all its complexities and contradictory realities.

Practical African-American theology and preaching also takes into account the "material spiritual-psychi-socio residue that permeates the life and experiences of those who stand at moments in human history with their backs against the wall."[66] In Dr. Moyd's paradigm of practical preaching and theology, the term practice does not adequately describe the magnitude of nonmaterial spiritual-psychi-socio experiences that African Americans face in their day-to-day struggles for redemption and social justice. He therefore applies the term *praxis* to encompass the wide range of behavioral and emotional experiences found in the context of African-American theology and preaching:

> Praxis is not synonymous with practice. Praxis has to do with the critical correlation or relationship between theory and practice. The correlation is dialectical. This means that theory and practice engage each other and are formed and revised by each other. The dialectical process is operative when theory negates practice and practice seems to negate theory.[67]

66. Olin P. Moyd, *The Sacred Art: Preaching and Theology in The African-American Tradition* (Valley Forge: Judson Press, 1995), 82.
67. Ibid.

Although Dr. Moyd's application of praxis to the African-American theology and preaching context has strong philosophical implications, he believes that this paradigm of praxis can and does involve the interactions of social and cultural groups with themselves and with others. Conceptually, he sees praxis as being the result of the actions of a person upon himself or herself and others in a group. Praxis is also believed to be the result of the actions of one group upon another group in a particular community or society. Praxis, therefore, argues Dr. Moyd is the "milieu out of which mores, practices, and institutions are formulated. It is a dynamic process in all communities and societies."[68]

When Dr. Moyd's philosophical paradigm of praxis is applied to African-American preaching, preaching can be viewed in both the material and the nonmaterial contexts. For it is a praxis that is born out of the concrete and abstract realities that African Americans are passing through at a particular time in their whole experiences in America. And since these realities can be seen in both the worship experiences and the feelings and aspirations of pilgrim people's struggle for redemption, it can be said that this praxis is undergirded with a redemption motif. For Dr. Moyd, the redemption motif gives rise to the structure of a practical theology—an applied theology—that empowers the African-American people to become actively involved with God in the redemptive acts of binding up the wounds of those who have been oppressed. This practical theology of redemption also informs the

68. Ibid., 85.

preaching task, because it directly and indirectly provides a template for assisting preachers and pastor-theologians who feel compelled to assist the underclass, the poor, and the marginalized to become involved in empowering and redemption. Caught in a social, political, economic, and even religious milieu of ontological absurdity, this practical theology of preaching and praxis could very well be a vehicle that can help lead oppressed people of all ethnic backgrounds to an affirmation of self-worth and personal being in the midst of human-caused nonbeing.

As practical theologians and preachers within this theology of praxis, we must be willing to view the hermeneutical enterprise through new and creative lenses. The age-old definition of hermeneutics as the theory of interpretation will not suffice as being universally binding when it is applied to the African-American context. While the African-American preacher and pastor-theologian may borrow from some of the existing hermeneutical language, the African-American preacher and pastor-theologian must apply new methodologies of interpretation if she or he takes seriously the Scripture with respect to the experiences of his or her listening audience. Dr. Moyd is correct in stating:

> It is precisely this African-American hermeneutic that has informed a practical theology, which informed African-American preaching, and which in turn has empowered an oppressed people.[69]

69. Ibid.

When preaching is informed by the folk rendition of African-American praxis, African Americans will begin to come to a self-understanding of their creation in the image of God. Indeed, they will be empowered to identify with the mysterious and the transcendence beyond the logical and the practical.

If African-American preaching is both material and nonmaterial, and if African-American preaching is derived out of an African-American praxis, then the context can provide the medium for the judicial hermeneutical approach for interpreting the meaning of God and redemption. This is the basis of Dr. Moyd's argument regarding the material and the nonmaterial, and his social and philosophical understanding of an African-American praxis. He believes that the central theme of African-American preaching that has made it so efficacious and empowering has been the redemption motif. For this concept not only has to do with the liberation from sin and guilt, it is also concerned with what God has done, is doing, and will continue to do in the life and history of a people on the underside of life.

The redemption motif can be seen and understood in the preaching context when those who have been victimized by racism and oppression are given the vitality to participate in their own healing. But this healing, both spiritual and material, must be undergirded by a practical theology, which will in turn inform the preaching context. Without a practical theology, it is likely that sermons will lose much of their force and impact as they are transmitted to the people. Indeed, those who are forced to swim against the tides of racism and other forms of human-caused suffering must hear sermons that help them to struggle against the odds, and to creatively engage in the redemptive movement. When both practical theology and preaching are inextricably united, theological interpretation will give essence to the preached message, and dynamic proclamation will empower the people. When African-American preaching is informed by an African-American theology, the preacher and pastor-theologian are able to go to the biblical texts more informed and with more hermeneutical options for addressing the needs of the people. Preaching can never be subjected to a hit-or-miss proposition; preaching is directed to a specific people, with specific needs at a specific time, and in a specific place.

As stated early on, the preacher and pastor-theologian must consistently ask himself or herself how can he or she best demonstrate to God's people through the proclamation of the Word the mighty and gracious acts of God. The preacher must also ask how he or she can best join together Scripture and the people's life situations in order to address their particular circumstances in a meaningful and practical manner. Dr. LaRue's "domain of experiences" becomes an instructive paradigm for looking at these questions both scripturally and experientially. Dr. LaRue defines a domain as:

> A sphere or realm that covers a broad but specified area of black experience and also provides a category for sermonic reflection, creation, and organization.[70]

70. LaRue, *The Heart of Black Preaching*, 20.

These domains of experiences include "personal piety, care of the soul, social justice, corporate concerns, and maintenance of the institutional church."[71] Dr. LaRue believes that an understanding of how these domains of experience find expression in African-American preaching can greatly assist preachers and pastor-theologians in learning how and what to preach to the many and varied life-situations in which African Americans find themselves. When these domains of common experiences are viewed with a belief in a powerful sovereign God who acts mightily on behalf of marginalized people, powerful sermons can evolve. These sermons will possess the theological integrity that not only addresses the salient themes of the gospel, but they will also take seriously the socio-cultural context of the African-American experience. When taken together, that is, theological integrity, cultural context, and domains of concrete experiences, the results can be powerful sermons that speak to the material and nonmaterial needs of the people.

One of the domains of experiences that Dr. LaRue lists is that of personal piety. Personal piety is thought to emphasize "heart religion," because it places a strong emphasis on the Bible for faith and life, the royal priesthood of the believer, and strict morality. Because of its rigid adherence to the Bible, it is believed that this domain may have emerged out of the evangelical movement of the late eighteenth century. Nevertheless, this domain of experience stresses clean hearts and righteous personal lives. Dr. LaRue argues that personal piety makes other demands on its adherents:

---

71. Ibid., 21.

> It emphasized the Christian life as essentially a personal relationship with God and Christ. It stressed the importance of the new birth (a profoundly emotional conversion experience) and how it ushered the converts into a new life of holiness, characterized by religious devotion, moral discipline, and missionary zeal. It rejected the appeal to reason in favor of a direct psychological assault upon sin with an equally direct offer of personal salvation. It dissolved the psychological and social distance between preacher and people, often evoking tearful, passionate outburst.[72]

It is clear from these descriptions of personal piety that this domain of experience is based upon a prior understanding of the Bible and the interpretation of the Christian faith. Preaching from this domain of experience clearly promotes moral and spiritual purity, but there is also the danger of placing too great an emphasis on the literal interpretation of the Bible. Those who preach from this domain must be careful that they are being faithful to the gospel and not promoting their own denominational partialities.

For those who preach from the "care of the soul" domain, emphasis is placed upon the well-being of the individual. While it has some similarities to the personal piety domain, the care of the soul domain places strong emphasis on the healing, sustaining, guiding, and reconciling of persons as

---

72. Ibid.

they face the changes of common human experiences. These are the experiences that are exacerbated in African-American life through systemic and capricious discrimination and injustice. Preaching from the care of the soul domain can aid those who need to overcome some impairment by restoring them to wholeness and by leading them beyond their own sordid state. It also has the possibility of guiding those who need help in determining what to do when faced with difficult problems and, therefore, must choose between various courses of actions. On the other hand, reconciliation is thought to help alienated persons establish or renew proper and fruitful relationships with God, family, and others. The function of sermons created out of reflection on the care of the soul domain experience, suggests Dr. LaRue, is to "salve or heal the wounds of the broken of life through some form of encouragement, exhortation, renewal, instruction, or admonishment."[73] This domain of experience presupposes that God will intervene in human affairs, empowering persons to withstand the stresses and strains of common human experiences. God is understood as being Protector, Sustainer, and Healer of the faithful, and His power is manifested in a mighty way to help the believer survive from day to day.

The "care of the soul" domain is predicated on the providence, omnipotence, and omnipresence of God who pervades the preaching context. Sermons constructed around this domain are designed to build an unshakable faith in the midst of the ups and downs of life. The African-American preachers and pastor-theologians who preach from this domain must be

---

73. Ibid., 25.

careful that they do not place so much hope on the distant future that they forget the existential here-and-now. The African-American believers must not be content with a worldview that everything will be all right after awhile. They must be led to believe that God is working on their behalf in the present.

The "social justice" domain is one that has received a great deal of attention from theologians like Cone, Wilmore, Roberts, and others in the last twenty or more years. This domain of experience includes those sermons that focus on social justice in a society where African-Americans are systematically discriminated against because of race. Yet, this domain of experience cannot be confined to racism alone, although racism is a major consideration where African-Americans are concerned. The social justice domain also includes caste, sexism, ageism, and other forms of discrimination. Those preachers and pastor-theologians who preach from this domain of experience presuppose that social justice is a basic value and desired goal in a democratic society where equitable and fair access to institutions, laws, resources, and opportunities are made available to all people. Racial justice is a form of social justice that emphasizes equal treatment of the races, a problem that has plagued the African-American church since its inception.

From a theological perspective, the social justice domain views God as the source of social justice. The African-American preacher and pastor-theologian interpret God as being all-powerful and, in turn, He gives them the courage to be ambassadors for social reform. Except for radical cases,

African-American preachers and pastor-theologians usually do not seek to overthrow the societal system per se; rather, they try to work within the system in order to bring about meaningful and constructive reform. They believe, as did the prophets of old, that God will support the principles of fairness and equality, and will make His power and love available in the present order to bring about fair and just treatment in systems and structures that negatively impact all people.

When God's power is made manifest in the social justice domain, it is directed toward what Dr. LaRue calls the "broader society." By this, he means that all of society is in some way, either directly or indirectly affected by the realities of social justice. Yet, it must be kept in mind that African Americans have suffered from systemic and capricious social injustice more than anyone in this country. While the problems and travails of other social groups cannot be taken lightly, African Americans are victimized more by these systemic and capricious social realities than others can imagine. As the African-American preacher and pastor-theologian construct sermons around this particular domain of experience, he or she should emphasize the fact that God's power can bring about large-scale changes and triumphs in this life as well as to some distant, otherworldly promise of vindication. This does not mean that the eschatological notion of vindication is excluded; what it implies is that God's power is at work bringing about change in the life of the underclass here and now.

However, the social justice domain has come under strong criticism by some African-American preachers and pastor-theologians who see personal piety and care of the soul as being preeminent in African-American preaching. They would argue that those who preach from the personal piety domain have been called out of the world to live lives separate from the present order. In their opinion, God's power is manifested in order to enable the believer to live an upright life that is above the cares and concerns of the secular world. Those who adhere to this view tend to take a literalistic approach to biblical interpretation. They are usually apolitical and see little to be gained from socio-political involvement at any level. In their opinion, the pulpit is not the place for political pronouncements, especially in the preaching context. Preaching from the social justice domain "kills the Spirit" in worship and weakens the witness of the church, they contend. In other words, the gospel transcends politics and race.

The corporate domain of experience includes some of the same concerns as that of the social justice domain. The major difference between the two is that the corporate domain tends to be more race-specific while the social justice domain tends to be all encompassing. While this domain of experience sees God's power being made available in the present order to bring about fair and just treatment for all people, including African Americans, the corporate domain recognizes that there are certain issues and interests that are specifically unique to African Americans. These unique experiences arise out of the cultural and social contexts that are indigenous to African-American life. For this reason, many African Americans, including some preachers and pastor-theologians, believe that African Americans best address matters such as self-help, self-determination, and racial solidarity. Like the social justice domain, the corporate domain is subjected to some of the same criticisms by some African-American preachers and pastor-theologians, namely, that it is too political and therefore has no place in preaching.

The fifth and final domain of experience is concerned with the maintenance of the institutional church. Clearly, the church is the place where many of the vital, life-altering experiences of the members occur. Those who preach from this domain of experience are usually concerned with those ministries and activities that go on within the fellowship. Ministries such as discipleship, missions, evangelism, Christian education, benevolence, and others find expression in this particular domain. Therefore, sermons constructed around this domain will tend to address the kinds of relationships required for spiritual growth and maturity. The sermons will also tend to address those issues that give continued life and sustenance to the institutional church, which in term reaffirms and upholds it members.

These five domains of experience place great emphasis on how the power of God is realized through various thematic considerations. These themes and/or methods, when applied to sermon preparation and interpretation, not only see God as being central, but also demonstrate what He is doing and how He is doing it. Dr. LaRue believes that these five domains of experience can accomplish the following goals:

> They can provide us with the means for understanding the common life experiences of blacks and avenues of core beliefs through which the

preacher may travel in an effort to connect God's power to the listener's concrete and tangible life situation. They also provide a treasure of sermon ideas and possibilities. [74]

What has been said so far regarding theological hermeneutics with respect to the African-American experience can be summarized in an analysis of one of Paul Laurence Dunbar's "An Antebellum Sermon." Upon review of Dunbar's early African-American sermons, one observes that a hermeneutical method emerges that can be applied, with some revisions, to modern day preaching and interpretation. Dunbar applied the method of contextualization, correlation, confrontation, and consolation. It is perhaps safe to say that Dunbar was not looking so much at method during the days of slavery as he was to content and meaning. Nevertheless, this paradigm allows us to see a common thread that ran through each sermon, and was remembered for its immediate effect and lasting value in empowering their hearers to live in the midst of oppression with faith and hope.

When one looks at the contextual component of these sermons, it is clear that they arose out of the early African-American experience of slavery and oppression. Whether expressed in literary or oral form, it was clear from these sermons that Africans Americans lived in a time in history where a dominant white society rejected, debased, and discriminated against them.

74. Ibid.

Indeed, the context of these experiences determined what was said, how it was said, and what was expected as a result of hearing the sermons. Although historical criticism, high and low, as a method of biblical exegesis and interpretation, was unknown to Dunbar at this time, Shannon concludes that he did in fact utilize the Scripture in its "synchronic and diachronic dimensions." The synchronic dimension would demonstrate how the biblical text was interpreted for those who lived during the time the text was written. On the other hand, the diachronic dimension demonstrated the relevancy of the text for those who had similar experiences across the centuries.

As a result of applying the synchronic and diachronic dimensions, Dunbar and other antebellum preachers and pastor-theologians were able to correlate the biblical text with the current conditions of their times. They were able to bring together the mutual and reciprocal relationships between text and context in creative ways that made the Bible come alive in an environment of servitude. While they were not predisposed to biblical criticism, these preachers and pastor-theologians did not confine themselves to a form of "biblicism," which interprets the Bible literally, nor were they guilty of "bibliolatry," the worship of the Bible as literally interpreted. Rather, their sermons reflected a sense of freedom and openness that enabled them to use figurative or metaphorical language as a way of explicating the text.

Through the principle of correlation, the antebellum preachers and pastor-theologians were able to provide the context in which the present hearer and the ancient hearer were brought together. Those who heard these sermons could readily see the relationship between the ancient oppressed people described in the Old Testament and the African Americans who experienced slavery and oppression. Just as the African Americans and the Israelites shared bondage and were subsequently redeemed, it was also believed that the slaves would eventually experience redemption. The principle of correlation allowed the early preachers and pastors-theologians to view the Bible as God's redemptive act of liberation and comfort on behalf of an oppressed people. What God did for Israel, he would do for African-American slaves.

While the principle of correlation allowed the antebellum preachers and pastor-theologians to look at the mutual and reciprocal relationships within the Bible, the principle of confrontation enabled these early African-American preachers and pastor-theologians to address African-American values and protest against oppression. These preachers and pastor-theologians made use of a linguistic device that Shannon calls "double entendre and humor." As a linguistic device, double entendre allowed certain things to be revealed to some people while disguising them to others. As a preaching tool, it proved invaluable for protesting the evils of slavery without alienating the white slave masters. In other words, the principle of double entendre allowed the preacher to confront the slave master indirectly while encouraging and strengthening the slaves. Shannon contends that the core of the message included the following:

God created humankind free. Slavery of any
kind of human bondage is against the divine
will. God is present in the human experience as
redeemer and Lord. God will destroy all forms
of evil and redeem those who have faith. [75]

In this particular sermon, the focus of the message presents
God as Creator, Redeemer, and Judge of evil. The preacher or
pastor's method of protest was not anthropological, but rather
theological. The battle was not between the slave and the
master, and it was not between the system of oppression and
the system of liberation. This sermon demonstrates that God
is the subject, not the predicate; he is the one who acts. The
battle is between God and evil, not between slave and master.
Because the battle is between God and evil, God will win, and
evil will ultimately be destroyed in their unique and creative
fashion, these antebellum preachers and pastor-theologians
made use of the principle of confrontation in showing the
relevance of the biblical Word in terms of divine creation and
liberation. They were able to provide consolation and
empower the slaves to deal with their daily insults and
burdens.

While the confrontation dimension provided the channel
through which the antebellum preachers and pastor-theologians could address both slave and master with the gospel, the
principle of consolation tended to be both pastoral and
redemptive. The immediate goal of these sermons was to
bring the good news to African-American slaves in distress.

75. Felder, ed., *Stony the Road We Trod*, 122.

The content of sermons was laden with words of comfort, condolence, encouragement, sympathy, and cheer from those who shared the same predicament. In a sense, it was a case of the wounded consoling the wounded by focusing on the deeds of God in history. On the other hand, the goal of these antebellum sermons was not only to bring immediate encouragement to those who were experiencing the abuse of slavery, but also to focus them on remaining vigilant and persistent in the midst of immeasurable suffering over the long-term. The sermons exhorted the African-American slaves to overcome the temptation to succumb to defeatism and escapism. These sermons not only provided the psychological motivation to persist in a "howling wilderness" of oppression, they also provided, above all, the faith in a God who redeems.

Based upon an analysis of context, correlation, confrontation, and consolation dimensions, we are able to see how Paul Laurence Dunbar's classic poem "An Antebellum Sermon" can be a resource for an African-American hermeneutic today. In the first place, the sermon is an example of African Americans telling their own story. It demonstrates how a major early African-American writer analyzed the language, scope, style, content, and method of the sermon to understand the hermeneutical principles applied by the preacher. The analysis of this hermeneutical method illustrates how the preacher and pastor-theologian were able to use the sermon to help African-Americans who suffered daily from chattel slavery.

Chapter 3 will examine the nature and character of God, as He is understood in African-American preaching.

Chapter 3

The Nature and Character of God in African-American Preaching

<hr>

Aim and Definition

The aim of this chapter is to examine the nature and character of God as He is portrayed in African-American preaching. Data acquired from interviews with various pastor-theologians will be analyzed and explicated in light of current thinking and reflection on the task of preaching.

The reality of God cannot be confined to theory alone in African-American preaching. While classical theological language is used to reflect on the nature and being of God, the preacher and pastor-theologian do not define and locate God in terms of who He is in some abstract sense. Rather, God is defined in terms of what He has done in history, past, and present, and what He will do in the future on behalf of those who stand with their backs against the wall. Those pastor-theologians whom I interviewed expressed these sentiments, either directly or indirectly, as they reflected upon how they interpreted the reality of God in their preaching. Therefore, whatever symbols or metaphors are used to talk about God, those descriptions will be more concerned with practical applications than they will be with orthodoxy in African-American preaching.

The Revelation and Creation of God the Father

Pastors Simms, Boston, and Hayes described God as the Creator of the cosmos and the Father of all humankind. Nevertheless, God is not understood to be only transcendent. Creator and Father are not only metaphors used to describe God as the source of all being who stands over and against all other finite or contingent beings. Rather, God should be understood as also being immanent, that is, He is believed to be directly involved in human affairs in all of creation. God is not only the creator of the cosmos; He also cares for all of His creatures. In this sense, God is said to "sustain and preserve creation generally and more particularly energize the wills and souls of the believers."[76]

For pastors Watson, Hayes, and Taylor, God providentially guides, sustains, and preserves human life by acting concretely in the affairs of existential realities. God is believed to be a way maker, a mind fixer, and a heart regulator. He is intimately involved, rather than passively involved in our lives. As the compassionate heavenly Father, God is concerned about His children. He desires that we live the abundant life, realizing our full potential with joy and purpose. The theme that occurred in many of the responses was that God is actively involved in the concrete affairs of people's lives, providing for their needs in unexplained ways sometimes.

76. Harvey, *Handbook of Theological Terms*, 147.

This brings up the question of revelation, that is, how these pastor-theologians understand the self-disclosure of God to be manifested in their lives and in the lives of those they serve. Revelation for some is understood both in terms of what God does, and the circumstances under which God brings about certain events. This is particularly true in light of the responses of some of the pastor-theologians who interpreted the manner in which they saw God acting. In some ways, these experiences seemed to have alluded to a mystical relationship with God. Yet, these experiences should not be interpreted in a magical or psychic sense where the person is believed to have had knowledge of God's spiritual truth through subjective experiences such as those of intuition and insight. Rather, these experiences should be understood as an act of grace where God's self-communication and revelation can best be explained by the Trinitarian doctrine. When these experiences are understood in light of Trinitarian mysticism, God's Trinitarian life is communicated by Jesus Christ through the Holy Spirit to the recipient. In African-American folk religion and thought, the mystical concept can be summed up in the statement: "God may not come when you want Him to, but He is right on time."

Thus, in the African-American Christian tradition in general and in preaching in particular, mysticism can be understood as God's revelation in the individual and corporate lives, and circumstances of the believers. In some ways, God has a way of showing up rather unexpectedly in the concrete affairs of our lives. For example, He revealed to pastor Hayes the steps to be taken in order to increase church growth when the membership was at a stand still. Through prayer and congregation participation, God provided the means for procuring financial resources for building renovations. As far as specific examples are concerned, these were the only two cited regarding God's revelation. The others tended to be rather general, citing only that God reveals Himself through events and circumstances. Although this sample of pastor-theologians represented a cross section of the major African-American denominations, males and females, their theological emphases were more toward the classical interpretation of God's disclosure. He is the compassionate heavenly Father who has revealed Himself in His Son, Jesus the Christ, and who is actively involved in reconciling and forgiving sin.

Only four of the pastor-theologians participating in this study addressed the social justice dimension that is so prevalent in black theology today. In C. Eric Lincoln's comprehensive study of the black church, he discovered that few ministers and laypersons were even aware that black theology existed as a discipline of study and reflection. However, it should be pointed out that Lincoln's urban data indicated that age, education, and denomination were the most significant variables in determining the responses. The following is a summary of his findings:

> Clergy who are forty and under claimed to be more strongly influenced by liberation theology than those who are older. Education was also very strongly associated with the knowledge of black liberation theology. Pastors with a high

school and less educational background said that they were minimally influenced by liberation theology, while those with a college 5 plus education have the most positive views of the movement. The majority of the less educated pastors have neither heard of the movement or the names of theologians associated with it.[77]

Lincoln cautions us that these findings should not be surprising, since liberation theology is a relatively recent intellectual movement occurring largely among the educated elite of the black clergy. These findings, along with the responses from the interviews of different pastor-theologians would suggest that the African-American preacher and pastor-theologian must not become locked into one particular theological formulation when talking about the revelation of God. To speak of God as Liberator is just one metaphor that the African-American preacher or pastor-theologian has at his or her disposal. He or she must also talk about the power of God in revelation.

The Power of God in Revelation

To say that God is all-powerful and that He is involved in our lives in very intimate and practical ways is affirming, but vague. And to say that God can do anything He wants to do

---

77. C. Eric Lincoln and Lawrence H. Mamiya, *The Black Church in the African-American Experience* (Durham and London: Duke University Press, 1990), 179.

in a general sense expresses the sovereignty of God. Perhaps it was the intent of most of these African-American pastor-theologians to be all encompassing in their responses about the power of God in revelation. Yet, it was clear from their responses that they believe that God acts powerfully in human affairs, even though they were not specific. Cone is correct when he says, "To ask who is God is to focus on what God is doing."[78] It is one thing to talk about the omnipotence of God in the theoretical and abstract sense, yet it is quite different to talk about him regarding existential realities. As African-American preachers and pastor-theologians, we are not only compelled to preach about God's power of liberation, emancipation from death-dealing political, economic, and social structures of society, we must talk about the power of God in other ways also.

LaRue argues for a "template" or a presupposition in which God acts mightily on behalf of the marginalized. By applying this concept to the power of God, he is able to describe the types of powers that are being revealed by God. One way of describing these types of powers is through the use of what he calls "extended metaphors." These extended metaphors allow the preacher and pastor-theologian to address such themes as liberation, deliverance, empowerment, providence, reconciliation, parenthood, and election within their particular context. By saying that God acts mightily, the preacher and pastor-theologian are not limited by any one theme or metaphor, but the use of several.

---

78. James H. Cone, *A Black Theology of Liberation*, (Maryknoll: Orbis Books, 2001), 27.

By using extended metaphors, it is possible for the preacher and pastor-theologian to move into the specifics of the sermon and begin to focus on the particular situation in which God acts. Instead of saying that God is actively involved in human circumstances, extended metaphors can provide the context for stating how and to what extent God is active in those circumstances. Indeed, God does not always act powerfully as Liberator; sometimes he acts mightily as Provider and Reconciler. LaRue believes that a God who acts mightily in a host of different situations provides more flexibility and is more inclusive of the extended metaphors that are likely to be found in the sermon. There is good reason to accept this statement especially when we see some of our colleagues, and even ourselves at times trying to fit a particular metaphor about God's power in sermons where they do not belong. Proctor, in "A Certain Sound of the Trumpet"[79] also cautions us against a one-dimensional style of preaching and calls for a broader understanding of the multidimensional aspects and needs of the African-American church.

It is possible for extended metaphors to provide great latitude, range, and flexibility for preaching in general and reflections on the power of God in particular. Yet, we cannot forget that African-American preaching and the historical and cultural context out of which it emerges is born out of oppressive suffering and dehumanization. Although African Americans have made some progress in race relations in the last forty or fifty years, they are still experiencing covert and overt racism

79. Samuel D. Proctor, *A Certain Sound of the Trumpet: Crafting a Sermon of Authority*, (Valley Forge: Judson Press, 1994), 16–18.

in this country. They are still the ones who are on the bottom end of the economic ladder. They are still the ones who are the last hired and the first fired. And they are still the ones who live in the worst of conditions in the urban centers. Indeed, African-American preachers and pastor-theologians must strive to be all encompassing in their preaching. In other words, they must strive to preach the whole counsel of God. Clearly they must talk about the power of God with respect to sin, guilt, forgiveness, reconciliation, parenthood, providence, and any other terms that are used to talk about God's power. Yet, the African-American preacher and pastor-theologian must address all of these extended terms within the context of marginalization and systemic oppression.

African-American preachers and pastor-theologians can ill-afford to forget their cultural and historical roots. They cannot forget how the old antebellum preachers and pastor-theologians approached Scripture and how they understood the ways in which God was active on their behalf. These antebellum preachers and pastor-theologians encountered in Christianity a powerful God, who throughout history demonstrated a willingness to side with the downtrodden in concrete and practical ways. As a despised and maligned people, the early African-American preachers and pastor-theologians believed that an all-powerful God was on their side. They believed that they found unconditional favor in the mighty sovereign's sight.

By no means does this suggest that God is not the God of all creation and that He does not care for all that He has made. Rather, African-American history and culture clearly show that an all-powerful God has not forgotten the powerless and the oppressed in the redemptive plan. These are the theological presuppositions that the African-American preacher and pastor-theologian must bring to the Scripture when he or she preaches about a God who acts mightily. At the same time, he or she must not become so one-dimensional in his or her theological reflections on the power of God that he or she forgets that those who come to church each Sunday are not only concerned about the failures of the institutions of society, they also need to be given the impetus to serve. They need education in religious matters and comfort in life's crisis moments.

In the words of Dr. Proctor, "The social prophet must remember the total menu and the need for a complete diet in the weekly sermon."[80] This statement is a sobering reminder that the universality of God is far greater than any theological formulation. Whether we are talking about God's power or any of the other themes pertaining to God's being, there needs to be, as LaRue argues, a "crucial balance in black preaching".[81] This balance may be brought about through constant reflection on the particular concerns of African-American theology with respect to God and the wider implications of the classical understanding of God.

---

80. Ibid., 18.
81. LaRue, *The Heart of Black Preaching*, 19.

The Justice of God

It is not only necessary that we talk about the power of God along with the concomitant metaphors that describe Him, it is also necessary that we talk about His justice or His righteousness within the context of capricious and systemic oppression. When the author presented the question of God's justice to the pastor-theologians, their answers ranged from those that deal with the classical understanding of God's justice to those of social justice.

In the first place, God is just, that is, He is right in all that He does, and He justifies those who by faith believe in Him. In this classical understanding of justice: justice and faith are inextricably tied to each other. The believer is declared right before God through faith that God grants to those who believe. This understanding of justice and justification leaves no grounds for boasting, as Paul states, because God alone initiates justice and justification. The hermeneutical principle with which this concept of justice is understood means that we are a people of faith, and this faith has both spiritual and ethical implications. As finite creatures, we are incapable of understanding all the ways of God, yet, He requires that we remain obedient and faithful. We do not understand why God allows some people to suffer dehumanization and systemic oppression, but these pastor-theologians believe, with few exceptions, that God is looking out for our best interest, and eventually, will work things out. In the interim, we are required to do good works toward others.

However, when we talk about the justice of God in the social context, God is already seen as acting on behalf of marginalized African Americans, especially when we look at where we were in history and where we are now. Even though some people of color believe that God is on the side of the rich and powerful, we are beginning to see some evidence to the contrary. This is especially true in the area of sports, particularly, in tennis and golf. There was a time, Pastor Horton contends, that these two sports were the sacred world of whites only. But now we see people like Tiger Woods and the William sisters dominating these two elitist sports. We only have to look back to the 1960s to see the remarkable social transformation that took place under the leadership of Dr. Martin Luther King Jr. to realize that God has not forgotten black folks. There was no question in the mind of Pastor Horton that it was the justice and power of God being played out in the concrete circumstances of African-American life that brought about these changes. Although the political and economic systems are designed to keep African Americans down, the justice and providence of God have raised and continue to raise them up time and time again.

It seems clear from these responses that the African-American pastor-theologians in the survey see the justice of God as being soteriological, social, and ethical. While God is concerned with the transformation of the inward person in relation to Himself, He is also concerned with the relationships that people have with others in society. It is not only important that human beings are reconciled and forgiven for their sins and guilt, it is equally important that human transformation is actualized in the ways we treat others who are the victims of racism, caste, dehumanization, and other forms of social injustice. The preacher or pastor-theologian who mounts the pulpit on each Sunday morning must come realizing that he or she has a responsibility to preach the whole counsel of God, which includes the justice of God. He or she must come realizing that God's justice cannot be limited to an either/or but rather a both/and proposition.

This is the reality that black theology must somehow reconcile. It must reconcile the classical interpretation of the justice of God and that which black theology advocates. In some ways black theologians have begun to reflect upon the nature of God's justice, along with other themes and characteristics endemic to God's self disclosure. For example, J. Deotis Roberts believes that we place the gospel in a situation of threat when we claim God's favoritism for us and distinguish between "we" and "they." If there is any sense in which we are chosen, he contends, it is for servanthood rather than favoritism. Even though God cares for the oppressed, the poor, women, children, and the aged, He also has a salvific concern for oppressors whoever they may be. Clearly, there are times when the oppressed become the oppressors. Therefore, black theology has an ethical task; it must be concerned about liberation, humanization, and reconciliation.

Black theology has a great deal to offer for the possibility of addressing the African-American situation. It has the potential for addressing the way other underclass groups reflect on the nature and justice of God. But first of all, black theology must cease to be the language of academia alone. It must make its way out of the classroom and become practical for the many African-American preachers and pastor-theologians who are not quite sure what black theology is all about. In addition, black theology must be willing to extend its meaning to be more inclusive of the other themes that relate to the justice of God.

Dr. Olin Moyd believes that the justice of God in black theology is inextricably intertwined with that of black redemption. In Dr. Moyd's thinking, the justice of God liberates African Americans and brings them into confederation with God and with fellow pilgrims. The concept of confederation presupposes that the justice of God not only sets human beings free from sin and guilt, it also sets them free so that they are able to stand upright before God in the world and live in community. This idea is totally different from that of the world view of relativism, where human beings, for selfish gains, prestige, and power, attempt to negate the justice of God and reduce other human beings to nonbeings. This is particularly true where African Americans are concerned. African Americans have had to live in a state of existential absurdity. In other words, they have and continue to be stretched between the poles of being and nonbeing, between the justice of God imputed to them on the one hand and the injustice of man forced upon them by other people.

African-American preachers and pastor-theologians who preach on the social justice domain of experience must not forget that justification in black theology evolved out of the African-American understanding of the justice of God in history. It is a history that constantly reminds us that the justification from above contradicts the setting in which we find ourselves. God's justice sets us free in ways that one is free while still held captive by systemic and capricious oppression. The justice that comes from above is the absolute justice of God that makes sense out of situations of existential absurdity.

This brings us to the idea of the wrath and retribution of God as they relate to the justice of God. The pastor-theologians did not address this issue directly. They did, however, talk about suffering caused by human beings. In the African-American context, the wrath of God is both individual and corporate. The wrath and retribution of God are the result of individual and collective sins. In the classical sense, God has granted human beings freedom. Yet, it is this same freedom that has led to alienation and estrangement from God, resulting in individual and corporate destruction. The wrath of God means that we are held accountable for our acts in this world and the world to come. Thus, the wrath and retribution of God are eschatological designations; they are both realized and futuristic. This means that the wrath of God has both existential and futuristic implications. It also means that the wrath of God cannot be separated from the justice and righteousness of God, which includes both retribution as well as undeserved forgiveness for our sins. For African Americans who have been and continue to be the victims of social injustice in America, the wrath of God means that the responsible parties will have to give an account for their actions. And since God is indeed an impartial and righteous judge, who does not discriminate between any racial or ethnic group, African Americans as well had better be careful how they behave in this world. For they too must give an account before the righteous judge who not only reveals his wrath, love, and mercy in this age but also in the age to come. The lines from an old Negro spiritual express this idea best: "You shall reap just what you sow. You shall reap just what you sow. On the mountain, in the valley, you shall reap just what you sow."

These lines, to a great extent, represent the theological expression of African Americans' understanding of the justice of God. God's justice is believed to have a built-in wrathful element that results in destruction of those who choose to conduct themselves in a manner that is contrary to the will of the Creator. It is a destruction that emerges out of a condemnation of the unjust. Paul Tillich contends that condemnation can only mean that the creature is left to the nonbeing that it has chosen.[82] And with reference to the wrath of God, he states:

> The wrath is neither a divine affect along side his love nor a motive for action alongside his providence; it is the emotional symbol for the work of love that rejects and leaves to self-destruction what rejects it. The experience of the wrath of God is the awareness of the self-destructive nature of evil, namely, of those acts and attitudes in which the finite creature keeps itself separated from the ground of being and resists God's reuniting love. Such an expression

82. Olin P. Moyd, *Redemption in Black Theology* (Valley Forge: Judson Press, 1979), 163.

is real, and the metaphorical symbol 'the wrath of God' is unavoidable.[83]

Dr. Moyd believes that Tillich is correct in his analysis of the wrath of God, but he feels that his assessment does not go far enough with respect to African-American thinking. While the work of love leads to self-destruction for those who resist it, the experience of the wrath of God is more than an awareness of the self-destructive nature of evil. Dr. Moyd argues that the wrath of God is grounded in African-American ontology, an understanding of the nature of being that gives meaning to life in the African-American community. In this understanding of ontology, the African-American religious community believes that God and His justice will bring down the oppressors and set the captives free, not symbolically and metaphorically, but in reality.

The assurance that African-American preachers and pastor-theologians are able to bring before their listening congregations is that God is just. We may not quite understand all of the suffering that African Americans have and continue to experience in America, as pastors Webb, Williams, and Hayes indicated, but God is still a just God. In the midst of both covert and overt injustice, it is the affirmation that the justice of God is not only transcendent, but that He is also immanent. The God of justice does not conform to some deistic idea of creation in which He creates a world and somehow does not providentially guide it or intervene in any way with its course or destiny. The African-American preacher and pastor-theolo-

83. Ibid., Tillich's work as cited in Moyd.

gian come with the assurance that God is immanent; that is, He intervenes in the concrete affairs of human existence and becomes personal in his actions.

God is just. This is the reframe that has occurred over and over in African-American life. It is the affirmation that under-girds much of the psychological and spiritual motivation for not giving up. This is what these pastor-theologians seem to be saying. Even though the howling winds of systemic evil continue to blow against a marginalized people, God is caring and provident. He is fair and impartial. Even though the culture of the privileged classes and the power elite may think that God is the enforcer or guarantor of the status quo, it is not only bad theology, it is dangerous for those who practice such beliefs. In the thinking of Dr. Henry Mitchell and Dr. Nicholas C. Cooper-Lewter, God threatens with justice those who break the social contract. He brings retribution on those who dare to contradict the common code, especially those who favor the class on top. On the other hand, this same divine quality is the hope of the have-nots. Justice is the limit that is placed on exploitation. It is believed to be the vengeance and vindication without which lowly lives would have no meaning. Therefore, it can be said that God's holiness and righteousness are synonyms for justice, and they are the bases for all guilty consciences, whatever the sin and among whatever sector of the population.

For this reason, African Americans have been more intense in their application of social justice because they believe that the God of justice is literally on the side of the poor and the oppressed. Just as Yahweh responded to the cries and groans of an oppressed Israel, He responds to the cries of a down-trodden and brokenhearted African Americans. The justice of God does not discriminate between people and therefore gives none the power to trample on the rights of others with impunity. "The law of divine justice surpasses the contrived human impediments and exploitative stumbling blocks manu-factured by even the highest arbitrators on earth."[84] Therefore, God's justice protects the downtrodden and the broken-hearted, and saves them from evil entrapments. He also confers meaning on their struggles in the interim, keeping them sane in the midst of crushing absurdities, as he brings them to victory in the end. Victory is believed to be certain because God defeats the enemies of the least in society. The hope of victory and vindication by a just God is one of the theological tenets that the preacher and pastor-theologian must continue to bring before a people who stand in need of spiritual and material liberation in this present age. The biblical witness provides the historical certainty of the current efficacy of divine victory by way of justice.

Indeed, the nature of the voice of God speaking out in full and perpetual presence is understood as an encouraging voice of liberation, both material and immaterial. The beauty of the voice of God accompanying the marginalized of society is that God's righteousness does not depend on our strength. In fact, our weakness is God's strength. Even in our efforts at seeking justice on our own, we find ourselves falling victim to indi-vidual and collective wills. Even though righteousness here on earth may stare us squarely in the face at times, and may even

---

84. Hopkins, *Down, Up, and Over*, 174–175.

be within our grasp, we may find ourselves stumbling. Thus, Hopkins argues for the idea of co-constitution of both human effort and divine effort. Because we are incapable of bringing about justice on our own, we need God to enter our concrete situations and carry us through. It is the presence of the divine vision toward liberation and community that breathes an invigorating energy for us to press on toward the higher calling of God.

Because God exercises absolute justice, He is absolutely free to bring about right relationships at any time, whether past, present, or future. This means that He is able to reach back into time, intervene in the contemporary time, and stretch forth the long arm of justice into the future. Because God is both omnipresent and omniscient, there can be no escape of his righteousness. Those who exercise oppressive powers over the weak and the dispossessed will suffer the presence of God's justice in this world and in the world to come, because injustice goes against the grain of God's onto-logical nature. It is evil and a curse on the created order.

Hopkins is right in stating, "The created ecology was orig-inally intended for peace and equal sharing of God's resources without a hierarchy of exploitation."[85] Only God sits high and looks low as is often repeated in many African-American sermons. And as a result of His sitting, the ethics, being, and knowledge of God are liberation for the poor and abused in society. Therefore, whenever and wherever injustice exists among people, it is an affront to God's nature of justice, a curse affecting the least in society, and a challenge against

85. Ibid., 177.

God. And wherever and whenever God sees this kind of injustice taking place, it compels him to act and to be on the side of those who suffer such injustices.

It is important to point out, however, that the presence of God's righteousness does not align itself with any particular sector of society, or because of any power or privilege that a particular sector may have. God is not on the side of African Americans because they happen to have a different hue from those of whites. He identifies with African Americans because they are the ones who suffer most from systemic and capricious oppression. He grants his righteous presence to the poor, the abused, and the locked out because God does not endorse evil. Injustice contradicts God's ethics, being, and revealed knowledge of divine intent. Knowledge of divine justice also requires us to fulfill the mandates necessitated by the struggle for liberation and confederation, which imply an ethics of justice.

For the African-American preachers and pastor-theologians, this means that the ethical dimension of justice and sanctification is the call to work out one's salvation with fear and trembling. It is a call for obedience, and also a call to faithfulness. This ethical dimension of justice is worked out in the community of the justified where redemption liberates the believer in the process of justification. The process of justification in turn brings the justified into confederation ("the forming of a community, local and universal, of the chosen people of God...") through the act of sanctification. The response of obedience and faithfulness is expressed individually and corporately in that it takes both to make up the confederation. In the case of the African-American church, the community—that confederation of African-American believers—is said to be the sanctified community working together with God, through faith, and with each other, moving as pilgrims toward the eschatological fulfillment of justification and sanctification.

The Mercy and Grace of God

Justification, then, is a gift. It is by God's mercy, love, and power that He causes the bright dawn of salvation to rise on us (Luke 1:78). It is God's mercy that His power is revealed to those who find themselves with their backs against the wall of secularism and relativism. God frees the captives and allows them to go free to live in ethical confederation with others who likewise have experienced God's mercy and power. For African Americans, this means that they have been freed to show mercy to others, even those who are guilty of racism, colonialism, sexism, and ageism. These are just some of the negativism that tend to separate people solely on the color of their skin, rather than on the content of their character. It may be that the God of mercy is calling upon African-American preachers and pastor-theologians to be the agents of redemption and salvation for an America that uses the forms and symbols of God, but denies the substance thereof.

The Bible is replete with incident upon incident revealing how God has raised up the least in society for the purpose of redeeming others. African Americans must be careful as God raises them to new heights of freedom that they too do not become the oppressors. African-American preachers and pastor-theologians must never forget that it has been the mercy of God that has sustained the marginalized on their way to freedom in space and in time. It has also been by the mercy of God that has enabled the voiceless to get over mountains of tribulation. "The emancipation process combines a co-constitution dynamic in which the divinity and humanity labor together for full spiritual and material freedom."[86] In addition to the mercy of an almighty God, Hopkins insists that the poor must maintain faith in the heart of the struggle to simply live daily and to gear up for the long-term journey. "Many times, given the sinister nature of race, class, gender, and sexual orientation, the least in society will endure trials and tribulations as a test of their faith in the Spirit of liberation for us."[87] Yet, it is through these trials and tribulations that we see the mercy and power of God being manifested on behalf of the afflicted of society.

The name El Shaddai means, "I am God Almighty," (Genesis 17:1) and He exercises absolute control over all of creation, and over one's spiritual and material life, whether rich or poor. Therefore, whenever and wherever the power and mercy of God intervenes in human affairs, His divine mercy grants power to those who are without power. Because God is who He is, it is impossible for Him to forsake the little ones who cry out to Him day and night. His omnipotence is always tempered by his compassionate mercy. So whoever engages in efforts to be with and at the service of the least in

---

86. Ibid., 180.
87. Ibid., 179.

society, whether black or white, will enjoy the gift of this all-powerful mercy.

In the final analysis, the justice and mercy of God are just two of the ways in which African-American preachers and pastor-theologians may talk about the grace of God. All that God does on behalf of the weak and the poor is because He alone chooses to do so. It is God's unmerited favor, reckoned as a gift that makes us right before a just and righteous God. Even the faith we possess, though suspect at times, is a gift of God. Hopkins' program of co-constitution emerges out of the preconditions for God's grace of salvation and liberation. The whole idea of co-constitution is "derived from the oppressed person's belief on the one hand, and the actual event of the divine working with the oppressed to realize salvation and liberation on the other."[88] In spite of the frailty of human effort, the grace of God is still capable of exhibiting a divine gift, on behalf of the underclass, whether it is progressive or reactionary. However, it is only through our faith in God's grace that total liberation and confederation are actualized.

It should be pointed out that God's grace has dialectical implications. Even though it is God's unmerited favor, it also comes with a price and a responsibility. The African-American preacher and pastor-theologian should never confuse cheap grace with that of costly grace. Dietrich Bonhoeffer understood the tension and the possible misconceptions that existed between the two concepts. He was careful to remind his countrymen of the potential dangers of being guilty of cheap grace.

---

88. Ibid., 181.

Bonhoeffer understood cheap grace to be "grace without a price; grace without cost! The essence of grace, we suppose, is that the account has been paid in advance."[89] Again, Bonhoeffer saw cheap grace as being an abstract quality:

> Cheap grace means grace as a doctrine, a principle, a system. It means forgiveness of sins proclaimed as a general truth, the love of God taught as the Christian "conception" of God. An intellectual assent to that idea is held to be sufficient to secure remission of sins. The church that holds the correct doctrine of grace has, it is supposed, ipso facto a part in that grace. In such a church, the world finds a cheap covering for its sins; no contrition is required still less any real desire to be delivered from sin. Cheap grace, therefore, amounts to a denial of the living Word of God, in fact, a denial of the Incarnation of the Word of God.[90]

Costly grace, on the other hand, "calls us to follow, and it is grace because it calls us to follow Jesus Christ. It is costly because it costs a man his life, and it is grace because it gives a man the only true life."[91]

Just as Bonhoeffer cautioned his fellow countrymen on the dangers of cheap grace, the author too would like to caution

---

89. Dietrich Bonhoeffer, *The Cost of Discipleship* (New York: Collier Books MacMillian Publishing Company, 1963), 45–48.

90. Ibid.

91. Ibid.

his fellow African-American preachers and pastor-theologians of the dangers of collapsing into a state of theological abstraction in their preaching on the nature and character of God. God indeed forgives us of our sins as a general truth. Yet, the intellectual assent to that truth is not totally sufficient to satisfy the concrete demands of costly grace. The hermeneutical principle of praxis requires the preacher and pastor-theologian to apply the grace of God to the existential realities that confront African Americans on a daily basis.

In other words, God's grace is not just a gift, it is also a language that speaks to us in words and symbols that we can understand. In the midst of existential absurdities, God's grace affirms our created self as good. Our racial and cultural identity is valued in the sight of God, because we too are created in his image, and therefore, we have no need to change our physical, cultural, or racial selves into something else. Costly grace compels every person who would proclaim the gospel to affirm and support the proposition that God's grace gives all people stewardship and protection over all the wealth, income and power in society. It is a collective gift for all people, especially those who find themselves on the underside of society. It is the promise that God will not leave the mistreated alone during any moment of the day. This is what the Negro spiritual means when it states that God constantly watches over us.

Costly grace is putting into concrete action God's holiness in diverse situations in the midst of a pluralistic society, both sacred and secular. There can be no separation between the sacred and the secular. If there was, "God's grace of freedom and liberation could become fractured, partial and provincial."[92] Yet, the sacred dimension embodies all of creation, and dwells especially in each vicissitude of the poor, the lonely and the weak. For this reason, God grants every person to be spiritually and materially free from those who exercise power over the disinherited. Indeed, God will leave no space, place, time, or event unchallenged or undisputed in the divine work that is necessary to make each individual and each oppressed community whole.

In addition, the grace of God can be understood as the energizing power that pervades the person of faith, because the action for freedom falls within the sphere of and is anointed by the effect of divine grace. Yet, it cannot be over stated that no human effort is capable of constituting a new self of freedom. Human effort takes on credibility only when it is viewed within the context of faith in God's freedom for us. In other words, there must be both the divine and human constitution of the liberated new humanity.

African Americans need to be reassured over and over again that they are not in the struggle of reconstitution and liberation by themselves. This would mean a contradiction of the grace and power of God. The lesson from Ephesians underscores this very fact:

> *"For it is by God's grace that you have been saved through faith. It is not the result of your own*

---

92. Hopkin, *Down, Up, and Over*, 184.

effort, but God's gift, so that no one can boast about it" (Ephesians 2:8–9).

This is what Hopkins refers to as a "mutual interplay between the faith of the oppressed in the grace of liberation and the freedom of God's gift of liberation."[93] In other words, no human action alone can yield the freedom of the new human being. "It is a co-constituting process with divine grace vivifying our embracing of faith and amplifying our efforts to be fully spiritual and material human being."[94]

Chapter 4 will deal with the nature and characteristics of Christology and pneumatology as they relate to African-American preaching and praxis.

---

93. Ibid.
94. Ibid.

Chapter 4

Christology and Pneumatology in African-American Preaching

Aim and Definition

Christology may be defined as "that area of Christian doctrine concerned with the revelation of God in Jesus."[95] According to Harvey, this has been traditionally expressed in the doctrine of the incarnation, the doctrine of the union of the divine nature in the one person.[96] "Christology is also reflection upon the one whom the Christian community confesses as Lord and Savior."[97]

In the African-American preaching tradition, Christology may be defined as that area of Christian doctrine that understands Jesus to be the one who not only saves us from our sins, but also liberates us from the suffering caused by human systems of oppression and social injustices. Jesus is the one who is preeminently celebrated in the preaching context. He is the one who is closer than a mother, father, sister or brother.

---

95. Harvey, *Handbook of Theological Terms*, 48.
96. Ibid.
97. Peter C. Hodgson and Robert H. King, ed., *Christian Theology: An Introduction to Its Traditions and Tasks* (Philadelphia: Fortress Press, 1985), 222.

In the African-American context, Jesus is not just a theological or a theoretical construct, He is Lord and Savior, a friend who acts concretely on our behalf.

Pneumatology, on the other hand is "concerned with that section of theology that deals with the works of the Holy Spirit." [98] According to Burrell, "the Holy Spirit is the promise of a new sort of life—at once a participation in the inner life of God and as activation of that divine image that each of us was created to display."[99] Burrell believes that the activation process is concerned with a kind of liberation that frees us from the posturing yto which we are all so prone, the pretense of autonomy. The doctrine of the Holy Spirit, he contends, shows us how that liberation takes place. It takes place by "the altering of our self-conception to become responders to the initiatives of God in our behalf. By articulating those initiatives as Father, Son, and Holy Spirit, the Christian tradition provides us with the abundant reminder of the inner life of God."[100]

In the African-American preaching context, the Holy Spirit is the abiding presence of the Lord with us; He is the one who dwells with us in the absence of the physical Jesus. The Holy Spirit enables the preacher and pastor-theologian to preach with power and conviction the gospel of Jesus Christ.

The aim of Chapter 4 will be to examine the Christological principles that inform the way in which African-American preachers and pastor-theologians reflect on the nature and character of Jesus within the preaching tradition. The

---

98. Harvey, *Handbook of Theological Terms*, 48.
99. Hodgson, *Christian Theology*, 326.
100. Ibid.

hermeneutical principles regarding the nature and character of the Holy Spirit will also be examined in order to determine the implications He has for the life of the believing community.

The Historical Jesus

The faith of the African-American Christian community and the preaching of African-American preachers and pastor-theologians are usually not preoccupied with a quest for the historical Jesus. They do not spend an inordinate amount of time trying to prove or disprove that Jesus existed at some time and place. This is the work of historical critical analysis. Rather, African-American preachers and pastor-theologians accept the biblical fact that Jesus is the fulfillment of the "I AM" of the Old Testament. Evans says that Jesus was a "figura."

> He was a cosmic reflection of Adam, the first-born, the image of God, as well as the historical reflection of Joshua, who led the Israelites into the Promised Land. Jesus was also a cosmic projection of the new Adam, the image of God restored to its original state, as well as the historical projection of liberated humanity, evident in the mystical/concrete notions of the church as the body of Christ and the people of God.[101]

101. James H. Evans, *We Have Been Believers*, (Minneapolis: Fortress Press, 1992), 78.

The use of the term *figura* was one mode of interpretation that allowed enslaved African-American Christians to see in Jesus an epic hero who embodied the values that promoted the liberation of the oppressed. The term also allowed them to see in Jesus a mediator who was concerned about their daily lives and survival.

Based upon both the interviews and the research, African-American preachers and pastor-theologians do not spend a great amount of time contemplating the humanity of Jesus. The Bible declares, however, that Jesus is the Son of God. He was born in a stable, wrapped in a blanket used for sick cattle, and His mother was a virgin of low estate (Luke 1:48). The angel Gabriel was sent from God to a city of Galilee named Nazareth, to a virgin betrothed to a man by the name of Joseph, of the house of David (Luke 1:26-27). Yet, in his humanity, Jesus was without sin. In fact, Jesus came into this world forgiving sin and promising eternal life to all of those who believed on His name. To the religious leaders of His day, Jesus was often viewed as a radical who resisted the traditions of normative religious practices. He caused friction between many of the religious and political leaders of His day. Yet, in some sectors of society Jesus was referred to as Counselor, Comforter, and Prince of Peace. In other sectors, He was found in constant conflict and confrontation with the priestly Sadducean hierarchy in the temple and the Pharisees who constantly questioned his authority. Nevertheless, the biblical record affirms that the man Jesus was a transformer of individuals in society. He preached a message of freedom and transformation to those who ventured to listen. "Through the parables, stories, and illustrations from the experiences of the people, Jesus taught his disciples and others the meaning of justice and fairness, truth and love."[102]

Howard Thurman, in his book, *Jesus and the Disinherited*, (might be considered a precursor to a more systematic articulation of Christology in black theology) reminds us that we cannot forget that Jesus was a Jew. He had a specific ethnic, racial, and religious identity. Hence, Jesus is identified within a socio-culture, socio-political, and religious context. Therefore, whatever is said concerning His humanity must be understood in terms of the sense of community that Israel held with God. As a Palestinian Jew, Jesus went about his Father's business, announcing the acceptable year of the Lord.

Jesus was not only a Jew of the noble class. Thurman believes that it was Jesus' condition of material needs that cemented His solidarity with the poor of His time. According to Evans:

> His poverty takes on added significance in the light of His designation as the human man, or the Son of man, because His economic predicament with which He was identified in His birth placed Him with the great mass of men on earth.[103]

Jesus could often be seen associating with the outcasts of society, befriending the most unlikely people of His day. Jesus

102. Harris, *Preaching Liberation*, 29.
103. Evans, *We have Been Believers*, 83–84.

spent time with people who were otherwise despised and ignored. "Jesus was a friend to tax collectors and sinners— those who were outwardly blameworthy and guilty of some of the things, about which we whisper and gossip."[104] Jesus was despised and misunderstood by the religious establishment because He did His work among those who were ostracized by the so-called good, respectable, religious people. Jesus did much of His work among the downcast, the nobodies of His day. Jesus went about doing good; "wherever He went, the sick were healed, the lame walked, the deaf were made to hear, the dead was raised, and the people heard the gospel preached to them."[105]

As African-American preachers and pastor-theologians focus on the humanity of Jesus, they must not forget to point to the obvious symbols of community in order to understand the hope, the need, and the possibility of change. When we consider the human conditions in the time of Jesus, we are sometimes amazed at the way He dealt with the persons He encountered. Lepers were feared, ostracized, and avoided. The blind were regarded as bearing the punishment for their own sins or someone else's. Harlots and publicans were thought to be beyond the bounds of the religious community. Yet, Jesus was a friend to all of them. Jesus saw people not in light of their failures, but in light of their personhood, significance, and their possibilities as children of God. Thurman observed two motifs that he believed to have been central in

---

104. Harris, *Preaching Liberation*, 30
105. Deotis, Roberts J., *Africentric Christianity: A Theological Appraisal for Ministry* (Valley Forge: Judson Press. 2000), 63.

Jesus' preaching. They include "the kingdom of God in us" and the prophetic manifesto from the prophet Isaiah that Jesus read in the synagogue: *"The Spirit of the Lord is upon me, because He hath anointed me to preach the gospel to the poor."*[106]

"The kingdom of God in us" presupposes the internal dimensions of salvation and liberation. Jesus is seen as "the Messiah" with all the Hebraic implications of the term. In this sense, Jesus may be referred to as "the Son of Man," the Liberator who has come to free oppressed humanity from the powers of sin, as well as the social structures that bear and breed sin. Here salvation is understood essentially to be sociopolitical even though "the Messiah" must also include the spiritual implications as well. The proclamation of Jesus quoted by Thurman, "The Spirit of the Lord is upon me, to preach the good news to the poor" is believed to be the touchstone for His position. Here the focus is on the external dimensions of salvation or liberation, and Jesus is the one who sets the oppressed free for the glory of God.

Thurman also focused on the notion of Jesus as "the Christ" with all the attendant Hellenized implications. Here, Jesus was first and foremost understood to be "the Son of God." In this capacity, Jesus acts as the "mediator between the forces of evil, the effects of sin, the forces of good, and the powers of redemption."[107] "The Son of God" motif understands salvation essentially to be spiritual, although it is not without sociopolitical implications. As "the Son of God," Jesus

---

106. Evans, *We Have Been Believers*, 85.
107. Ibid., 86.

the Christ is the one who saves us in both spiritual and material terms, in both the religious and the social dimensions of life. The incarnation points to the facts that "the Son of Man" motif identifies Jesus "the Christ" as the mediator of God the Father. 'He is the one who has broken down the barriers that we have erected between God and ourselves and others, thereby saving us from isolation and alienation, which is the lack of community that is the real experience of death.'[108]

As African-American preachers and pastor-theologians, the Bible also reminds us that Jesus was a member of an oppressed minority. Indeed, He shared the sense of outrage that came with the domination of the Palestinian Jews by the Roman Empire. This was the inescapable social and political context of Jesus' maturation. The New Testament is replete with instances where assassination attempts were made on His life. Yet, because His time had not come, He removed Himself from life-threatening situations. Clearly, suffering and oppression were not uncommon in the life of Jesus and His ministry. He lived and suffered the injustices of hate and even death on the cross. African-American preachers and pastor-theologians have historically understood the way Jesus was treated as an example of unmerited suffering, and they have identified the suffering of African Americans during the period of slavery, Jim Crowism, and covert racism with the suffering of Jesus.

There are those who unjustly refer to the African-American faith as that of Jesusology because of its strong Christological emphasis. It cannot be disputed that much of African-American preaching has a Christocentric focus, because many

---

108. Ibid., 96

preachers and pastor-theologians close their sermons by recounting the event surrounding the crucifixion, death and resurrection of Jesus Christ. Proponents of this view contend that the entire African-American sermon is built around this much-anticipated celebrated moment.

It has been this writer's experience that while many African-American preachers and pastor-theologians do close their sermons in this manner, there is good justification for the Christocentric argument. First of all, one must realize that the fate of Jesus is completely in the hands of God. Within the crucifixion story, the power of God is made manifest when God raises Jesus from the dead. This is the moment of celebration. This is the Christocentric moment for both the African-American church and the preacher. No matter how eloquently or profound the preacher or pastor-theologian says it, the crucifixion and death of Jesus will not have its full impact until the preacher proclaims that early Sunday morning, God raised Jesus from the dead. Jesus did not rise on His own; He was raised by the power of God. LaRue writes:

> No one who hears the complete story can deny that the preacher or pastor-theologian is also celebrating the redemptive power of God manifested on behalf of Jesus, the crucified one.[109]

Hence, the resurrection demonstrates the power of God to overcome death on a cross by raising Jesus from the dead. Indeed, the death and resurrection of Jesus are the basis of the

---

109. LaRue, *The Heart of Black Preaching*, 112.

Christian faith and hope in African-American preaching. It is the faith that has sustained African Americans from slavery to the present. The African-American preacher and pastor-theologian celebrate the death and resurrection of Jesus because they feel that the resurrected Jesus has come to live within their souls. Therefore, the enthusiasm that usually accompanies their testimony is evidence that the resurrected Jesus is also constantly affecting the resurrection within the individual. Moyd contends that the individual is not only resurrected from death and the state of sin, he or she is also being resurrected from the circumstances of human oppression.

Jesus the Liberator

For African-American preachers and pastor-theologians, liberation is inextricably intertwined with the death and resurrection of Jesus Christ. Liberation means the emancipation of the marginalized and underclass from oppressive and capricious systems of social, economic, and political injustices. Liberation also means the forgiveness of sins and reconciliation. Within this particular context, liberation has a dual function: on the one hand, it has sociopolitical implications, and on the other, it is essentially spiritual. For some African-American preachers and pastor-theologians, Jesus is the one who stands in the midst of an oppressed people, and brings relief to them on behalf of God. He is the champion of the poor who comes to the aid of those on the sidelines of society.

While pastors Monroe and Table emphasized the social dimension of Jesus' liberation mission in the world, the other pastor-theologians concentrated on the spiritual aspects of liberation. Here, liberation and salvation tend to coalesce. In this respect, God's love is clearly seen in the person of Jesus, in that He sent Him into the world in order that we might have abundant life. No matter what we may be going through, Jesus still loves us and will make Himself available to those who diligently seek Him. He is the source of our hope, joy, and peace.

The hermeneutical principle of liberation also has ethical implications. We are required to do unto others what we desire to have them do unto us. Through His atonement, Jesus reconciles us to Himself and brings us into confederation with fellow believers. The Spirit of confederation or community places us in the position of being concerned for others. Our full humanity is directly tied to others attaining their full humanity. Jesus was always suspicious of those who were more concerned about their own aggrandizement. Proctor writes:

> Even though Jesus encouraged thrift, planning, and even investing for profit, yet He was suspicious of the rich of His day. Jesus did not congratulate the man for building bigger barns and the rich ruler on his success.[110]

Jesus was fully aware that the wealthy could not be fully human unless they shared their wealth with the poor, thereby

---

110. Samuel D. Proctor, *How Shall They Hear: Effective Preaching for Vital Faith* (Valley Forge: Judson Press, 1992), 74.

making all equal in relation to God's created resources on earth. Whites cannot be fully human until African Americans, Native Americans, Latinos, and other underclass social groups are given equal access to the wealth and institutions of society. When African-American preachers and pastor-theologians preach on the ethical principles of liberation, it is important to call attention to the illusions that have been created by the dominant social group. According to Proctor:

> The distinction created by poverty and historic exclusion and isolation means more than they do. Beneath such distinction, all persons are equal. When we acknowledge this equality, we authenticate other persons who have been so victimized."[111]

Black Theology and Liberation

Olin Moyd provides a rather comprehensive definition and description of black theology in his book, *Redemption in Black Theology*. He understands black theology to be:

> ...the Black community's attempt to reflect upon the historical relationship—events—between God and themselves. It is the Black community's attempt to describe those events in the clearest and most coherent language at its disposal. Black theology is the Black community's attempt

---

111. Ibid., 67.

to articulate its understanding of "what in the world God was doing" or "what God was doing in the world" while Blacks were undergoing slavery, Jim Crowism, second-class citizenship, the struggle for "integration," and the strides for Black power, Black identity, and social justice. Black theology seeks to explicate the Black community's understanding of God's promise and the goal toward which he is directing the world while Black people in America are and were going through dehumanizing experiences.[112]

Black theology is also concerned with the liberation of African Americans from disabilities and constraints brought on by human systems of oppression. It has been indicated already that black theology is primarily the discipline of the academy. It is primarily black theologians' talk about God within the context of academia. Although a few African-American preachers and pastor-theologians are beginning to include black theology as a necessary part of their preaching agenda, especially the younger and more theologically trained preachers and pastor- theologians, it has not received the attention that some African-American theologians believe it deserves. Black theology is the black theologian's method and mode of reflecting upon the Christian faith with respect to the Christian community, and therefore something must be said about black theology in relation to Jesus and liberation.

112. Moyd, *Redemption in Black Theology*, 23.

The questions that immediately come to mind when we talk about black theology and liberation with respect to the life, death, and resurrection of Jesus Christ are: Should black theology become the sole theological paradigm for African-American preachers and pastor-theologians' preaching about Jesus? Or, is black theology just another resource made available to African-American preachers and pastor-theologians for preparing sermons that speak to the concrete needs of African-American people? While there is a common socio-political thread that runs through the heart of black theology, black theologians tend to differ somewhat in their emphasis on certain aspects of the liberation theme. James Cone, for example, sees liberation as God with the oppressed; Dwight Hopkins analyzes liberation from the concept of the co-constitution of the new self and community; Olin Moyd looks at liberation in terms of redemption not only from sin, but also redemption from "human-caused" suffering; and J. Deotis Roberts views liberation with the idea of reconciliation. The scope of this book does not allow for an in-depth analysis of each of these theologies. However, a summary of each theological program hopefully will provide helpful insights relative to black theology's place in African-American preaching about Jesus the Christ as Liberator.

Like classical theologians such as Ernst Kasemann, Gunther Bornkamm, Hans Fuchs, and Hans Conzelmann, African-American theologian, James Cone, takes the quest of the historical Jesus seriously also. He believes that it is important to know whom Jesus was in order to know who He is for African Americans today. Cone writes:

"Without some continuity between the historical Jesus and the kerygmatic Christ, the Christian gospel becomes nothing but the subjective reflection of the early Christian community."[113]

Black theology, on the other hand, holds that the historical kernel is the manifestation of Jesus as the oppressed One whose earthy existence was inextricably related to the oppressed of the land. For Cone, this is critical to the understanding and the appropriation of the historical Jesus. The failure to identify Him with the poor is to misunderstand Him and thus distort His historical person.

The hermeneutical principles underlying Jesus' birth, baptism and temptation, ministry, death and resurrection are understood to be identified with the oppressed of society. "His messiahship meant that He was one of the humiliated and the abused. In His baptism, Jesus identified His existence as one with sinners."[114] And by doing so, Cone believes that He conveys the meaning of the coming kingdom. According to Cone's hermeneutic, "The kingdom is for the poor, not the rich; and it comes as an expression of God's love, not judgment. In His baptism, Jesus embraces the conditions of sinners, affirming their existence as His own."[115] Through Jesus Christ, God breaks into human history primarily on behalf of those who are poor, weak, and abused. The announcement that the kingdom of God is at hand seems to

---

113. James H. Cone, *A Black Theology of Liberation: Twentieth Anniversary Edition* (Maryknoll, New York: Orbis Books. 2001), 112–113.

114. Ibid., 115–118.

115. Ibid.

send a clear message to those who would enslave others that the pre-eminence of God's rule has come to replace every false authority. Jesus represents the inauguration of a new age in which God Himself has taken on the plight of the oppressed, and invites their full participation in the kingdom-building process. This does not mean that Jesus was not concerned for the wealthy or that there were rich people who did not have noble spirits. Joseph Arimathea, for example was a rich man (Matthew 27:57) and was "a good and righteous man" (Luke 23:50). Although Zacchaeus offered to give back only half his possessions, Jesus took into consideration the attitude with which the gesture was made. Clearly, Jesus was concerned about all people, especially those of the underclass and the helpless.

This principle takes on added significance in the death and resurrection of Jesus Christ. For Cone, the hermeneutical principle underlying the death and resurrection of Jesus is the freedom of God who takes on the totality of human oppression. The revelation of God's freedom in the death and resurrection of Jesus is not dealt with in light of the Atonement where God was in Christ reconciling the world to Himself. Rather, the death and resurrection of Jesus demonstrate without question that God is not defeated by oppression. He contradicts and reverses the notion of human infinitude by transforming Jesus' death and resurrection into the possibility of liberation. The proclamation of the death and resurrection of Jesus can now be reinterpreted in a new light. The fear of death need no longer be a factor in our standing up against the systemic evil of oppression. Jesus has liberated the oppressed from the fear of death. In Christ Jesus, we have been set free to live without worrying about social ostracism, economic insecurity, or political tyranny.

Liberation for Dwight Hopkins bares some of the same qualities and characteristics as those of Cone's. Hopkins, however, approaches liberation from the standpoint of the co-constitution of the new self or the new humanity with Jesus, the liberating Spirit. Hopkins sees the underclass and the marginalized working together with Jesus Christ, through faith, to bring about spiritual and material freedom. He begins with the inaugural sermon preached by Jesus in Luke 4:18–19 that is taken from Isaiah 61:1–3. In these verses, Jesus declares:

> *"The Spirit of the Lord is upon me, because he has anointed me to preach good news to the poor. He has sent me to proclaim release to the captives and recovering of sight to the blind, to set at liberty those who are oppressed, to proclaim the acceptable year of the Lord."*

Jesus enters the social location of the people of faith who are at the bottom of society in order to bring good news and good tidings to them. Jesus comes to repair broken hearts that have been fractured by wicked spiritual powers on earth. Hopkins writes:

> The intent to proclaim liberty to the captives denotes a holistic salvation and liberation encompassing the entire dimension of the poor.

> The bursting asunder of prison doors suggests both metaphorically and literally how Jesus removes the poor from all manner of prisons and prevents them from struggling for liberation and practicing freedom.[116]

Also, associated with the verses from Luke 4:18–19 is what Hopkins refers to as a "freedom calendar." This freedom calendar has futuristic implications in that the acceptable year of the Lord enjoins the poor to respond to the divine gift of Jubilee by conducting themselves as though new Common Wealth has arrived. However, the divine gift is not without cost. Everyone must go before the bar of judgment day, the day of vengeance. Rich and poor, blacks and whites, and peoples of all colors and situations of life must submit their lives to an accounting. "Did they or did they not strive to co-constitute the new life with Jesus—the Spirit of total liberation with us now."[117] Did they co-constitute the new spiritual and material humanity here on earth by bringing about justice for the poor and weak in society? These questions, Hopkins believes will be the nature of inquiry at the judgment bar of Jesus.

The death and resurrection of Jesus Christ also play a major role in Hopkins' concept of co-constitution of the new humanity. Similar to the thinking of Cone, Hopkins believes that Jesus' death and resurrection represent His victory over the death of poverty and pain, which is also linked with his

---

116. Hopkins, *Down, Up, and Over*, 195.
117. Ibid.

concept of the atonement. Since Jesus has overcome poverty and sin, African-Americans and other working people can have the hope that a difference has not only been made in the cosmic realm, but also in their daily lives. They are also given the courage to pursue a vision in which their lives and the lives of their children will be free to attain their full potential as human beings.

Hopkins also includes the hermeneutical principle of *voice* as part of co-constitution and liberation. Hopkins' use of the word *voice* refers to "the autonomy that the poor and marginalize now have in expressing their own needs and concerns." Jesus' death and resurrection have not only brought about the act of reconciliation in the classical sense; they have also freed the poor to assert their own voice with all their might. For those who have been the victims of systemic and capricious injustice, they do not have to acquiesce to the voice of those who oppress. The co-constituted new humanity with Jesus Christ now realizes that the oppressor's voice is not their voice, a misconception that the poor and oppressed have been led to believe for so long. The profound tragedy of such a misconception is that those on the underside of society have been exploited and discriminated against to such an extent that they become participants in their own exploitation and discrimination. And "all the time the victim thinks that he or she lives in freedom and not in the shadows of a deadly system, both spiritually and materially, personally and systematically."[118] Yet, "thanks be to God through Jesus Christ," there

---

118. Ibid., 210–212.

is a new voice that comes as a result of the co-constitution of a new humanity with Jesus.

The African-American preacher and pastor-theologian, therefore, have the opportunity and the responsibility to be a voice of co-constituted liberation on the path toward practical freedom. African-American preachers and pastor-theologians who support the status quo in their preaching and interpretation may not only be guilty of participating in inadvertent oppression (spiritually and materially), they may find it difficult to open themselves up to receive the ongoing manifestation of Jesus for the new humanity. They cannot perceive of a female pastor-theologian having anything to say about the good news of freedom. Those who support the status quo in preaching and interpretation may fail to connect the appearance of the Spirit of liberation to the Bible, the knowledge that the same Spirit of liberation can come from the least in today's society. African-American preachers and pastor-theologians and pastor-theologians of different cultural groups cannot afford to have a truncated approach to the Christian faith, no matter what nationality they may happen to belong. Truncated faiths and stifling theologies limit Jesus' revelation to His ascension. No one has the power to contain the omnipresence of Jesus' liberating Spirit. And no one can close the canon on where Jesus chooses to be. In Hopkins view, Jesus' resurrection from the dead signifies the ongoing hope of Jesus' presence with them."[119]

Olin P. Moyd's Christology locates Jesus as the "Redeemer of humankind from this worldly state and circumstances that

---

119. Ibid., 217.

diminish the fullness of His people as well as Redeemer of humankind from sin and guilt."[120] His analysis of Jesus as Redeemer takes into consideration both the horizontal and the vertical dimensions of redemption. The horizontal dimension is concerned with Jesus as the one who liberates human beings from suffering that is caused by other humans. "And the vertical dimension is concerned with the liberation (saving) of humankind from their sins and guilt arising out of their acts of spoiled or broken relationships with the Source of their being."[121] Redemption in African-American thought has and continues to be preoccupied with the classical aspect of redemption as Moyd rightly points out. "Jesus is the one who brings fallen humanity and sinful human beings back into a right relationship with the eternal, and the atonement took place on the cross of Calvary."[122] As a rule, African-American preachers and pastor-theologians have not engaged in extended theological debate on the subject of Docetism. They generally do not engage in philosophical speculations on how one man could atone for the sins of all, or to whom the ransom was paid. And they do not spend an inordinate amount of time trying to determine why it was necessary that a human life was sacrificed in order that God might redeem humanity from sin and guilt if God is all powerful and could have wrought human salvation by some other means. African-American preachers and pastor-theologians accept the biblical rendering that Jesus did in fact die on a Friday afternoon, and

---

120. Moyd, *Redemption in Black Theology,* 131.
121. Ibid, 133.
122. Ibid, 134.

was raised early one Sunday morning. There is a common testimony that can be heard in the African-American church, which says:

> I know that my Jesus died on Calvary for my sins. I know that He was buried, and I know that on the third day He rose from the grave; how do I know? Because He rose in my soul.

Music in the African-American church has and continues to play a major role in affirming the spiritual and material implications of the death and resurrection of Jesus. The old Negro spirituals and gospel songs speak of His life and death, suffering and sorrow, love and judgment, grace and hope, justice and mercy. Jesus' death and resurrection are reflected in these songs, and can be heard on any given Sunday morning resonating throughout African-American congregations. Indeed, they contextualize every aspect of life that African Americans experience.

"I Want Jesus to Walk with Me" is a Negro spiritual that is often heard in the African-American church. Moyd argues that this song had a double meaning, as many of the Negro spirituals had. On the one hand, Jesus is seen walking with the people through the wilderness of oppression, and on the other, He walks with them through the world of temptation and evil. "In one way Jesus would walk with them as a political Redeemer; in another way Jesus would walk with them as a spiritual Redeemer."[123]

---

123. Ibid.

This spiritual, like so many others, expresses the complete trust in and the dependence on Jesus to be with African Americans in the concrete existential experiences of their life struggles. African-American preachers and pastor-theologians realized that the pilgrimage through this physical life was and continues to be a difficult task. The African-American preacher and pastor-theologian must not only beseech Jesus to walk with the listening audience, he or she has a compelling need to have Jesus to walk with him or her in an effort to proclaim the gospel of redemption and salvation. Unfortunately, many African-American preachers and pastor-theologians are still experiencing some of the same social injustices that their members are facing. Like their members, they too find themselves trying to survive at the level of being human under inhumane circumstances. Both pastor and people realize that they need a power greater than that which they can muster from natural, physical, mental strength. So they invoke Jesus to walk with them through the howling winds of systemic evil, because they know that Jesus knew what it meant to be downtrodden. Jesus was numbered with the downtrodden. Therefore, both pastor and people know that Jesus knew what it means to be beaten without a cause, because He too, was beaten without a cause.

This is the knowledge that keeps hope alive for the African-American church community. It is the belief that its people will ultimately triumph victoriously over trouble caused by secularism, relativism, and oppression. As one gospel song states:

Victory, victory shall be mine,
Victory, victory shall be mine,
If I hold my peace
And let the Lord fight my battle,
Victory, victory shall be mine.

This gospel song expresses both patience and assurance. The forces of evil cannot be defeated through violent confrontation, because the enemy is far better equipped. But if we will just hold our peace, Jesus will ultimately bring victorious hope, freedom, and justice in this "one nation divided." Jesus will fight our battle in spite of the fact that we struggle in a nation thwarted by the powers that cause much pain and suffering to those who are weak and defenseless. Yet, spiritual and material victory shall be ours because the preacher and pastor-theologian come with a word from the Lord each Sunday morning, declaring that victory is certain.

J. Deotis Roberts, however, believes that Christology and ecclesiology are the two important doctrines that must be considered when talking about liberation theology and Black theology in particular.[126] In Roberts' opinion:

> The very nature of a theology concerned with liberation from oppression and reconciliation among those to be set free requires a careful examination of Jesus and His church.[125]

---

124. Roberts, *Black Theology in Dialogue*, 43.
125. Ibid.

In the African-American Christian church, it can be safely said that Jesus is the glue that holds the church together. A reexamination of Christology and ecclesiology is needed in the first place to make sure that the Jesus of history is given due attention as well as the Christ of faith. And since ecclesiology deals with the importance of fellowship and community among those who are oppressed, it too must be given equal attention, according to Roberts' Christological analysis of liberation.

For African-American preachers and pastor-theologians who preach from Roberts' Christological analysis of liberation, they must understand that he is concerned with both liberation from oppression and reconciliation in the world. It is also important that they understand that Roberts sees the church as an extension of the incarnation of Jesus Christ. In a world experiencing spiritual and material bondage, and estrangement, both personal and social, the church is "at once a healing balm and a word of judgment."[126]

The Holy Spirit

While African-American theologians have not paid a great deal of attention to the doctrine of the Holy Spirit in their reflections on black theology and liberation, the Holy Spirit is not lacking in the preaching by preachers and pastor-theologians in the African-American churches. According to those pastor-theologians whom the author interviewed, the Holy Spirit is

126. Ibid., 51.

absolutely essential within the preaching context. As the third person of the godhead, Pastor Hayes indicated that the Holy Spirit is the one who energizes and empowers our preaching. Without the anointing of the Holy Spirit, the preacher or pastor-theologian is merely speaking words that have no meaningful impact on the lives of the hearers. But if the Holy Spirit is indeed present within the preacher or the pastor, the sermons will have power to motivate people and to transform their lives. Even though they may not be able to understand the mystical nature of the Holy Spirit, those who experience Him will know that a change has taken place in their lives.

In the absence of the physical Jesus, Pastor Table indicated that the Holy Spirit is the assurance that Jesus is with us, just as the pillar of cloud led the people of Israel by day and pillar of fire by night. Pastors Hayes, Monroe, Webb, and Horton understand the Holy Spirit as being our helper, the one who comes to our aid when we are in bondage and protects us in our deliverance. The Holy Spirit is the one who walks with us and talks with us. He is the one who applies the Word of God to our daily lives. Through faith, He calls into existence those things we cannot see.

In a sense, it may be said that the preacher and the Holy Spirit are partners in the proclamation of the gospel. The Holy Spirit is seen as the intangible force that hovers within and around the preachers and pastor-theologians in order to encourage them to keep pressing on. When confronted and challenged by the injustices of the modern Pharaohs, Herolds, and Pontus Pilates of today, it is the Holy Spirit who gives strength and power to the sermon in ways that no human initiative can imagine. Harris is right when he contends that "after study, prayer, writing, singing, and doing everything else to prepare ourselves for the task of proclamation, our weakness prevent us from being totally ready to preach."[127] Yet, when the time comes for proclaiming the gospel of Jesus Christ, the Holy Spirit empowers the preacher and pastor-theologian in his or her weakness.

The African-American preachers and pastor-theologians are called upon to confront the issues of injustice and oppression, as well as individual sin and reconciliation. In order to bring about spiritual and material transformation in individuals and in society, African-American preachers and pastor-theologians need all the power they can muster. They need that same Spirit that descended upon Jesus on the day in which he was baptized; the same Spirit that compelled Jesus to proclaim that He had been anointed by the power of this Spirit to speak words of liberation to those who had ears to hear and eyes to see; and it was the same Spirit that allowed Peter and the other disciples to proclaim the gospel with boldness in the midst of threats and persecution. That Spirit is none other than God in Christ with us. He is that mystical presence whom Pastor Hayes asserted that, "He walks with us and He talks with us, and assures us that we are not alone in life's struggles."

Some mainline African-American protestant denominations have and are following the thinking of many of the white mainline Protestant denominations regarding the function of the Holy Spirit. Their contention is that physical healing, prophecy, and tongues were limited to the age of the apostles

---

127. Harris, *Preaching Liberation*, 34.

and the early Christian church. Yet, many African-American churches, especially those of the Pentecostal tradition see the gift of speaking in tongues as a major tenet in their Christian faith.

It cannot be denied that African-American theologians have not given the same attention to the doctrine of the Holy Spirit as they have given to the doctrine of God and Christology. Indeed, more theological reflection and dialogue are needed in this area, especially where the preaching task is concerned. We need to have a better understanding of the works of the Holy Spirit in the African-American community of faith. It may be helpful to revisit Moyd's theology of redemption where we not only are concerned with the liberation from suffering, but we are also concerned with those spiritual and ethical qualities that will make us a confederation of reconciled people and, by the aid of the Holy Spirit, will empower us to break down the walls of hatred and injustices.

Following are conclusions for each of the previous chapters.

Conclusions

The following conclusions have been reached for each theological category cited within each chapter. Each theological category has been explicated in light of its implications for preaching in the African-American context. In each chapter, materials from previous research and from pastor-theologian interviews have been brought together in order to determine what the nature and content of a theology of preaching in the African-American context may become.

African-American Religious History

It was apparent from my interviews with various pastors who were of different denominations that a theology of history plays a major role in how and what they preach. Pastors Simms, Monroe, Webb, Williams, and Table referred to such books of the Bible as Genesis, Exodus, Joshua, the Psalms, and the Gospels in order to illustrate how God acted in ancient history on behalf of those who struggled against oppressive structures. In Genesis, these pastors said they found the promises of God to a marginalized people. In the book of Exodus, they are able to relate the struggles of an oppressed Israel to that of the early African slaves and modern day racism. In the book of Joshua, they see how God fights on behalf of those on the underside of society. In the book of Psalms, they see how the people of God are able to celebrate in the midst of suffering, knowing that an omnipotent and omnipresent God will eventually deliver them from their enemies. And in the gospels, they see Jesus Christ standing with and taking the side of the dispossessed. While these books were used almost exclusively in the days of slavery, Pastors Simms and Watson warned that we should be cautious about concentrating on specific books in this day and time, since all of Scripture contains some instances of God deliverance and redemption. Failure to consider the entire Scripture can lead to ignorance and anti-Semitism.

It was also pointed out that during the period of slavery, it was illegal for slaves to learn to read and write, therefore, their preaching lacked "doctrinal foundation." Specifically, they were referring to the Epistles of Paul whose writings are those of the teaching variety as opposed to the narratives. However, this should not be interpreted to mean that antebellum preachers and pastors were not theologically relevant. Their limited understanding of the Bible simply prevented them from reflecting systematically upon the text. Yet, the need for a better systematic understanding of doctrine and theological reflection is incumbent upon African Americans and other preacher-pastor-theologians who would proclaim the gospel today.

Yet, the general consensus of those pastor-theologians who participated in the interviews was that knowledge of African-American history was paramount for effective and relevant preaching. Without knowledge of our past, as Pastor Horton suggested, we have no sense of our identity as a people of struggle in neither the present nor any anticipation of the future. It is within the scope of African-American history and the Bible that we are made aware of our liberation in time and space. Liberation was predicated on the generosity of either a white political orientation, or the skills and intellect of some black folks. Clearly, it was the hands of a loving God acting through whatever human agencies and events He chose in order to bring about redemption and liberation.

Theological Hermeneutics in African-American Preaching

Hermeneutical principles become quite instructive and revealing when they are seen in tension with pastor-theologians who devote the greater part of their time and energies to ministering to their respective African-American congregations. The African-American pastor-theologians whom the author interviewed identified three areas or methods that they considered to have been critical in the interpretative process: the historical context, the cultural context, and the biblical context.

The historical context consisted primarily of a history of interpretation based upon the biblical text. Pastors Simms, Horton, and Hayes were convinced that any effort to do theological interpretation must be done by Scripture alone. Their understanding of hermeneutics did not take into consideration the historical or the cultural contexts. In other words, Scripture interprets Scripture as far as these pastor-theologians were concerned. Therefore, any history of interpretation must begin and end with the Bible. Any talk about what God is doing in the world today must be understood in terms of what the God of the Bible has done in the past and will continue to do in the future.

However, when African-American pastor-theologians go to the Bible, they must be careful that they do not become guilty of spiritualizing the text. They must be careful that they do not impose their own theological interpretation where such an interpretation is not intended. Rather, the pastor-theologian must be cognizant of the place, time, and situation that a particular statement was made and why that statement was made. In addition, the pastor-theologian should have an understanding of the language and geography of the people being studied.

Although most of these pastor-theologians took a rather literal approach to the history of interpretation where the Bible was concerned, it appears that some if not all of them believed that the synchronic and diachronic dimensions of interpreting Scripture were preeminent. Through looking at a text in terms of language, geography, time, space, and circumstances, they are able to interpret the biblical text for those who live during the time the text was written. Through looking at these historical variables, they could in turn, determine the relevancy of the biblical text for those who are experiencing similar conditions.

It must not be denied that the Bible is central for both preaching and theological reflection. However, today's preachers and pastor-theologians cannot forget or ignore the fact that the African-American antebellum preachers and pastor-theologians interpreted the Scripture in ways that were relevant for their times and indeed, for our time. They have passed on a tradition of biblical interpretation that is invaluable for those of us who dare to understand and preach the gospel of Jesus Christ to those who are victims of social injustice, racial discrimination, caste, and other forms of social maladies. We must be willing to hear not only the voices from the ancient past, we must be attentive to those eighteenth and nineteenth century African-American prophets who interpreted the Bible in light of their cruel reality of existence.

These pioneers of the African-American struggle in America brought new meaning and insight to the Bible. Unlike some of their white counterparts in the United States who tended to interpret the biblical events more theoretically, African-American pastor-theologians tended to interpret them more literally and concretely. Although they did not know anything about biblical criticism, yet they read and interpreted the Scripture in light of their own existential realities. The Bible came alive for them as they identified their own oppression with the historical characters of the ancient text.

It must be kept in mind that the early pastor-theologian's world view evolved as a direct result of reading the Bible or hearing the Bible read. Scriptural discrimination was not the result of manipulating or spiritualizing the text under consideration; rather it was the earnest attempt of the preacher to bring together those passages of Scripture that spoke to the struggles of that day.

Indeed, Scripture must be allowed to interpret Scripture, as those pastor-theologians suggested. The biblical text is first and foremost the ground and starting point for any analysis of interpretation. However, contextual preaching for the African-American pastor-theologian will require that she or he be willing to look through some new and modified lenses of biblical interpretation. When we say Scripture only, we have an obligation to ask "whose?" If African-American hermeneutics is going to be contextual, as it must, it will require that African-American preachers and pastor-theologians be willing to unload much of the traditional theological baggage that has been dominated by Western thinking. The African-American pastor-theologian must be willing to reinterpret, revise, and undo much of what have been spoken and written by Western theologians. Those African-American pastors who mount the pulpits each Sunday morning must come to realize that no theology of preaching or otherwise is universal and normative for all people, times, and conditions.

We must look at Eurocentric traditions of biblical interpretation with guarded suspicion. This means that we owe it to ourselves as pastor-theologians and to those we serve, to examine with critical integrity the theology and history, and the culture that have dominated African-American thinking.

In African-American preaching, we talk about "making it real" or "making the sermon live." What these phrases mean in hermeneutical language is that the preacher and pastor-theologian must make every attempt to address the socio-cultural, socio-political, socio-economic, psychological, and spiritual needs of the members of his or her congregation. The African-American preacher and pastor-theologian who are determined to make preaching relevant for today's awaiting congregations cannot forget that his or her sermons are derived out of situations in life. And these situations in life cannot be fully understood unless the preacher and pastor-theologian take into consideration the total context in which his or her preaching takes place.

The Nature and Character of God in African-American Preaching

Both the responses from the pastor-theologians and the writings of Moyd, Hopkins, Proctor, Roberts, and others show that the abstract realities of God are not sufficient for African-American preaching on the nature and character of God. Classical theological language is used to reflect on the nature of God's ontological nature. Yet, the African-American pastor-theologian is more concerned with the spiritual transformation of the person. They are also concerned with what God has done in history, past and present, and what He will hopefully do in the future on behalf of those who suffer from systemic and capricious injustice. Creator and Father are not merely symbols and metaphors used to describe God as the source of all beings who stands over and against all other finite beings. Rather, God is understood to be immanent, and is directly

involved in human affairs in all of creation. Hence, God providentially guides, sustains and preserves human life by acting
concretely in the affairs of existential realities.

Those who preach on the revelation of God should realize
that revelation is not just a theoretical term used to define
God's disclosure in the academic sense. In the African-
American context, the people who sit in the pews each
Sunday morning want to know what in the world God is
doing, or what is God doing in the world, and under what
circumstances is he doing it.

How God is active may sometimes take on mystical conno-
tations. Yet, mysticism should not be interpreted in a magical
sense; rather, the experiences associated with such phenomena
should be interpreted and understood as an act of grace
where God's self-communication and revelation are best
explained in light of the Trinitarian doctrine. God's Trinitarian
life is communicated through Jesus Christ and through the
Holy Spirit to the recipient. Thus, in the African-American
Christian tradition, mysticism can be understood as God's
revelation in the individual and corporate lives and circumstances of the believers.

For the most part, these pastor-theologians were more
influenced by the classical interpretation of revelation. God is
the compassionate heavenly Father who has revealed Himself
in His Son, Jesus the Christ and who is actively involved in
reconciling and forgiving sin. Only pastors Horton, Table and
Boston addressed the social justice dimension that is so prevalent in black theology of liberation. This is not surprising, as
Lincoln observed, since black theology is a relatively recent

intellectual movement occurring largely among the educated elite of black clergy. It is the author's contention that black theology has much to offer to African-American preaching and practice. It is the one discipline in which African-American preachers and pastor-theologians can reflect systematically on the Christian faith within the context of the African-American experiences. We do great disservice to the people whom we serve and even to the gospel when we become one-dimensional in our theology and in our preaching. Indeed, black theology can become the vehicle by which we as African-American preachers and pastor-theologians reflect upon the Christian faith. Yet, black theology has the responsibility of addressing the whole counsel of God.

For those of us who preach predominantly from an African-American tradition, we too must realize that our talk about God cannot be an either/or proposition; it must be both/and, lest we too become guilty of theological discrimination. God is not on the side of the poor, the weak, the underclass, the marginalized, and the oppressed because their skin complexion happens to be different. God identifies with this sector of society because God does not endorse evil, and injustice is an affront to His nature.

Christology and the Holy Spirit in African-American Preaching

African-American preachers and pastor-theologians are primarily concerned more with the spiritual and ethical dimensions in their Christological reflections than they are about the social, economic, and political dimensions. This does not mean that they do not address social, economic, and political issues in their sermons. It means rather, that their preaching is preoccupied more with the spiritual transformation of the inward person. They seem to echo the sentiments of Evans who contends that Jesus called all people to a higher right-eousness through a spiritual revolution and transformation. The true revolution of Christ was essentially moral and secondarily social, economic, and political.[128] Jesus' messi-ahship, His pronouncement of the kingdom of God, and His death and resurrection were intended to usher in a new age where He would become the mediator between sinful humanity and God. Jesus did not come to sanction a particular cultural group or one system over another. He was owned by no one, and belonged to no particular group; He was the Son of man, the Son of God who was vitally concerned about the spiritual transformation of all people—black, white, yellow, red, and every color in between.

Black theologians, such as J. Deotis Roberts, James H. Evans, Dwight Hopkins, and Olin P. Moyd have taken signifi-cant steps in reconciling the social and spiritual dimensions in their black theological reflections. Clearly, they have recog-nized that their theological programs must not only talk about Jesus as the one who liberates from social injustices, but also the Jesus who liberates us by transforming our minds and our souls. The African-American preacher or pastor-theologian must keep these two hermeneutical principles in constant tension with each other if they are to preach sermons that are

128. Evans, *We Have Been Believers*, 87.

existentially relevant for those who come to hear a word of hope each Sunday morning. African Americans need to know that Jesus not only walks with them in the midst of their day-to-day struggles of life; they also need to know that He walks with them in the midst of their guilt, their estrangement, and their reconciliation.

The African-American preacher or pastor-theologian also needs the aid of the Holy Spirit. In the absence of the physical Jesus, the Holy Spirit is the assurance of Jesus' presence with them in their preaching and in other areas on their ministries. Yet, African-American preachers and pastor-theologians must not only be concerned with the doctrine of the Holy Spirit in the classical sense, they must also apply those concomitant hermeneutical principles that give concrete meaning to this doctrine.

Those who are endowed with the Holy Spirit are empowered to stand with bold confidence in the midst of systemic evil and declare the justice of God through Jesus Christ. Just as the prophets and apostles of the Old and New Testaments were empowered to address the critical issues of their day, African-American preachers and pastor-theologians too, have been granted the same power. They have not only been called and ordained by God, they have been granted the mystical power to bring about spiritual and material transformation to those who co-constitute themselves with Jesus Christ for a new humanity.

With the exception of the question on the justice of God, only Pastors Table and Monroe addressed the social justice problem as a hermeneutical principle contained in the other theological questions. Clearly, this problem did not go away with the passing of the sixties and seventies; nor was it resolved with the small gains made by some African Americans. Many African-American males and females are still victims of racial discrimination in job hiring, housing, and educational opportunities.

It is this author's contention that many of the African-American preachers and pastor-theologians have not given serious consideration to what prominent African-American theologians have written on black theology and its implications for preaching. Until they do, African-American preaching will continue to miss out on a vital resource that can help them address the critical issues and problems that confront the people whom God has called them to serve.

Appendix A

Questionnaire

1. Who is Jesus in African-American preaching?

2. Who is God in the preaching experience?

3. Who is the Holy Spirit in the preaching experience?

4. How is your understanding of God made meaningful to your congregation?

5. Which books of the Bible do you feel best address the conditions of the African-American church?

6. What connections, if any, do you see existing between the life issues that members of your congregation face and the kind of songs that are sung in the preaching context?

7. To what extent do earlier African-American preachers influence how and what you preach today?

8. How are God and Jesus Christ preached where the African-American male is concerned?

9. How does the history of African Americans in this country inform the content of your preaching today?

10. How do you preach about justification and sanctification in the midst of oppressive social, economic, political, and religious systems?

11. Do you tend to preach more from the Old or New Testament, and why?

12. To what extent is your preaching informed by the political and social issues of your congregation?

Appendix B

Descriptions of Pastors Interviewed

Pastor Simms

Pastor Simms is a recently retired pastor of a small Baptist church in the Mt. Airy section of Philadelphia. Pastor Simms was the pastor of a church that was predominantly African American, although he did have a small number of white members. Pastor Simms has been an ordained minister for forty-six years, and he has served three pastorates during his thirty-nine years of ministering. Pastor Simms is seventy-four years of age, and has four earned degrees; one of which is a Doctor of Ministry degree.

Pastor Williams

Pastor Williams is a recently retired Presbyterian pastor who was the pastor of a small suburban Presbyterian Church in Delaware County. Pastor Williams' church was a racially mixed congregation consisting of about sixty percent whites and forty percent African Americans. Pastor Williams has been an ordained minister for eight years, and he was a pastor for nine years. Pastor Williams has served three pastorates. He is sixty-seven years of age, and has earned three degrees; one of which is a Master of Divinity degree.

Pastor Boston

Pastor Boston is the pastor of a medium size United Methodist Church in the Germantown section of Philadelphia. Pastor Boston's congregation is made up primarily of African Americans. He has been an ordained minister for thirty-four years. He has served as a pastor for twenty-seven years; and he has served four pastorates. Pastor Boston served as the pastor of the historic Zoar United Methodist Church prior to assuming his present pastoral position. Pastor Boston is also active in civic affairs. He serves as a member of the Board of Education for the Philadelphia School System. Pastor Boston is fifty-one years of age, and he has earned a Master of Divinity degree along with other graduate studies.

Pastor Hayes

Pastor Hayes is the pastor of a medium size African Methodist Episcopal Church in North Central Philadelphia. Pastor Hayes has been an ordained minister for approximately twenty years, and she has served as a pastor for approximately fifteen years. Pastor Hayes has a very viable ministry in the heart of North Philadelphia, as she continues to come up with creative alternatives for meeting the pressing needs that face her members and the community. This is the only church

Pastor Hayes has pastored. She is fifty-five years of age and has a degree in biblical studies.

Pastor Mann

Pastor Mann is the pastor and founder of a growing medium size Baptist Church in West Philadelphia. After leaving his previous pastorate, Pastor Mann took less than a hundred members and built a new edifice. Pastor Mann has been an ordained minister for twenty-three years and has been a pastor for seventeen years. He is fifty-one years of age and has been the pastor of two churches. Pastor Mann has a degree in biblical studies and is presently completing the requirements for the Master of Divinity degree.

Pastor Monroe

Pastor Monroe is the pastor of one of the largest African-American churches in the Philadelphia area. His membership consists of over three thousand members. Pastor Monroe's Church of God in Christ is located in the Mt. Airy section of Philadelphia. Pastor Monroe has thirty-four ministries in his church designed to meet the specific needs of his congregation. He has been an ordained minister for forty years, and has been the pastor of this church for thirty-six years. This is his only pastorate. Pastor Monroe is sixty-nine years of age. He attended the Philadelphia College of the Bible.

Pastor Table

Pastor Table is the pastor of a small Baptist church in the Fern Rock section of Philadelphia. Pastor Table is a strong social and political activist in the community and in the ministerial environment where he is president of the Black Clergy. Pastor Table has been an ordained minister for thirty-one years, and he has served as a pastor for sixteen years. This is Pastor Table's second pastorate. He is sixty-two years of age and has a college degree.

Pastor Webb

Pastor Webb is the pastor of a thriving medium size Baptist Church in West Philadelphia. Pastor Webb's congregation consists of all African Americans. He has been an ordained minister for sixteen years, and has pastored this church for sixteen years. Pastor Webb holds offices in both the state and national conventions. He is fifty years of age and has a college degree.

Pastor Watson

Pastor Watson is the pastor of a relatively large Baptist Church in Southwest Philadelphia. His membership consists of over eight hundred members. Although the membership is predominantly African Americans, he does have some white members. Pastor Watson has been an ordained minister for thirty-two years and has served as a pastor for approximately fifteen years. Pastor Watson is fifty-five years of age and has served two pastorates. Pastor has a Doctor of Ministry degree.

Pastor Horton

Pastor Horton is a retired pastor of a small Baptist Church in Southwest Philadelphia. He has been an ordained minister for fifty-eight years, and has been a pastor for forty years. Pastor Horton is held in very high esteem by fellow clergy, as he spends a great deal of his time helping younger pastors acquire a better understanding and appreciation of the pastorate. Pastor Horton is eighty-three years of age and has been the pastor of three churches. Pastor Horton is also seminary trained.

Appendix C

Transcript of Interviews

1. Who is Jesus in African-American preaching?

Pastor Table

Jesus is the preeminent celebrant of our preaching. Jesus is the very Son of God who provides for us a holistic salvation. So when the African-American preacher takes to the pulpit, he is proclaiming the Christ of the Bible, the One who is the Son of the living God. So fundamentally, Jesus becomes the standard bearer of the oppressed people and for people who had experienced slavery. Consequently, when we come together to hear from God, we are anticipating what the salvation message is that Jesus brings. In Old Testament language, Jesus is the One who comes to set the captives free.

Jesus is our celebrated hero who brings relief to the oppressed, addressing the people on behalf of God. He is the One, whom God has sent and into the promise land, as He did for the Israelites. Jesus also brings us to a land flowing with milk and honey. Jesus is the celebrated person with whom we identify.

Pastor Simms

I'm not too sure, I get the impression that some of the men don't seem to know that He is God, and they preach about God, but Jesus Christ is God who became a man.

Pastor Monroe

I approach this from two perspectives. In my mother and grandmother's day, Jesus was seen more as the Savior to give us salvation. At times that is wonderful and glorious, but I think in this modern day the African Americans look at Him as our liberator. The emphasis that is put on Jesus now is the one who is the champion of the poor, who comes to our aid, liberates us from the sidelines.

Pastor Webb

I present Jesus, the Lordship of Jesus Christ, as Lord, Lord of every situation of our lives. He is in charge and ruler of our lives. Rather than as the babe of Bethlehem, or the weakest hour at Calvary, I might go through that because I always present Him as Lord. He should affect us in our daily lives and rule our lives so there are some limitations that affect my everyday living because He is Lord.

Pastor Watson

I want people to know, in every sermon that I preach, even if its not a text concerning the life of Jesus, that Jesus is God in flesh and that God loves us enough that He sent His Son into the world so that we might have an abundant life and to know that in spite of how their life is going, Jesus loves them. And He is available to all that seek Him, and will forgive them of their sins. We have an opportunity to establish a close relationship with God. As people see Him operating in our daily lives, people see Him daily. If I know that Jesus loves me, and because of that, I know He is forgiving. In Him there is hope, joy and peace. That will affect my relationship with other people and will affect how I operate on my job, in my community, and with my family and people I love. We look at life with a different perspective when a person believes that they have access to God's grace.

Pastor Hayes

I interpret Jesus as the Son of God and the second person of the trinity. Jesus is key to all of what we preach and teach, because He bled, died, and suffered for all mankind; not only for us, but for generations passed and generations to come. I try to get people to understand that Jesus is the answer to all our problems, directly or indirectly. I believe that if you put your faith, confidence, and trust in Jesus Christ, that through His Holy Spirit He will reveal to you whatever He wants you to know about whatever it is. I teach that He is Lord and unless He becomes Lord of your life and He directs you to whatever you are going into, then you are going to fall and be directed by someone else who is anti-Christ. I believe that we have to know in our churches that the Lord is the reason for all we do. So I preach Him in all that I do.

Pastor Williams

Jesus is the Son of God. And is God, the Word in the flesh. He came into the world to save humankind. He is the light of the world and shows the path from earth to glory. To show obedience to God and the love for all people, Jesus came to save us from our sins. He died for our sins on the cross. So whatever challenges we face in this life, through Jesus Christ, we can have success. Jesus Christ is divine, and yet human; therefore, Jesus did suffer and was able to experience life as we experience it. He understands and He shows us that all things are possible if we give it to God and follow God's direction and His purpose for us in our life. The love of Jesus provides us with God's love. God's Word is our teacher and the only way to salvation and victory.

Pastor Mann

Celebration goes back to the beginning that God is, even in Jesus Christ, in the death, burial, and resurrection of Jesus Christ. It is essential to exalt the Christ after a sermon. I think it has much to do with style in African-American preaching, and it comes out of what has preceded. I have never seen a 747 jet plane lift up, but it has to go on the run way before lifting up. So a sermon has a runway before it reaches the altitude to land on the runway for the pastor and people to enjoy the ride.

Pastor Boston

Jesus is the Son of God, our Elder Brother, who has already walked where we are to walk. And He has modeled the way that we are to follow and is with us in our present day walk and is with us to encourage and to support.

2. *Who is God in the preaching experience?*

Pastor Table

We see Him as Father, as the all-powerful One, as being involved in our lives in a very intimate and practical way. Personally, we talk to God in our preaching in a very personal way. We see Him as our Holy Father, the One whom we address through prayer, who knows our circumstances. We expect Him, as the Psalmist says, to hear our cry and deliver us as He delivered Israel with Moses. We have names for God by which we identify with Him. The Jews called Him Jehovah Salom, El Shaddai, and Elohim. We say that He is a heart fixer, mind regulator, One who supplies our daily needs. Our expressions are very pictorial. For example, Jesus Christ came from God from heaven in human flesh to set people free. While our foreparents may not have had the ability to read the Bible, they said, if any man believes in Jesus Christ, he is a new creature old things are passed away as recorded in I Corinthians. If the preacher understood that, he had to pictorially explain that to his congregation, to men and women who may have been slaves and who were illiterate. The expression, I looked at my hands and they looked new, my feet and they did too. They could understand and see that, and what was read from the Scriptures became a picture to help them identify with God (more concrete than abstract).

Pastor Simms

The Creator, Father, Son and Holy Spirit are all the same. He is the one who blesses the Word in our teachings; not our sermons, but His Word. God is center, as He has affected our lives and what He has done in our lives. The Holy Spirit is a preaching experience. I think since we are Christians, and He lives in the preacher, in our bodies, we are to rely on Him to use His Word as promised. His Word is not null or void. Some of our preachers try to work up the Holy Spirit, and that's not ideal for our hearers. Just let Him have His way in our preaching. Remember, it is His word, the survival and honored by the Holy Spirit.

Pastor Monroe

I am presenting Jesus as the compassionate Father that is concerned about His children, God of forgiveness, God of love, of compassion, and of understanding.

Pastor Webb

I present God as the first person of the godhead, the omnipotent, meaning that He is everywhere, present at the same time. There is a saying, He sees all you do and hears all you say. That should affect the things we say and do and how we treat one another because He is God and He is everywhere.

Pastor Watson

I try to present Him as Jesus presented Him, that is not in the abstract, but through Himself, we look at Jesus and see

God. So God becomes a living reality who is present with us in our daily activities and every day lives. We hear of a reference that Jesus "is the man upstairs" but that is not true because He is not somewhere else. He is not like the Greek gods and disconnected with our human affairs; not in a cold or callous way. God then becomes spectator, but in our Christian faith, God is present and with us; not just in worship on Sunday, but always in our daily activities. He also wants our good, for us to live abundantly (whatever that means), not necessarily material things, but live lives joyfully, fulfilling, and with purpose.

Pastor Hayes

We focus more on Jesus Christ than we do on God, and so what I have been doing is preaching who God is. A few Sundays ago I preached "God is Good," in order to let the people know that God is good and is the owner, the creator and the sustainer of all life, and because He allowed His only begotten Son to die for the sins of all the world. It expresses the love God has for all humanity. So people have to understand that God is the Father and that Jesus Christ is the Son and the Holy Spirit is the third part of the trinity.

I teach them that God is there for us and God gave His most precious gift for us. Just as He was revealed in the Old Testament, God reveals Himself, even today; even on 9/11 at the World Trade Center. God didn't do it, but He allowed it to happen to get the attention of the world because people have forgotten that God is the Creator and people have allowed other idols to come into their lives, and especially Americans.

They have been so blessed with so many material things until their things have become their God. So God is saying to America and the world that I am still the God of the universe and of all things.

So mankind must know Jesus Christ and the Holy Spirit and never forget God. And the church must never forget God. The church has forgotten God and is so busy with their social issues and problems, their fashion shows and chicken dinners, etc. They are focusing on other things. They have forgotten God and who gave them life and the purpose for which the church was established/founded. I believe that we have many of the problems today because we have forgotten God. Single parents, mostly women, have to raise these children without a father image. How are they to know God? If they knew God then they could make and could understand that God the Father is with me. I may not have an earthly father and my mother may be a single parent, but if I have God in my life, then He is my Father. But many of our children don't know that and because they have not been taught how to identify with God the Father, they can't identify with an earthly father. Even when single mothers marry, it is difficult for those children to accept a father into their lives, but if they had been introduced to God the Father in their lives then they would have fewer problems. He is loving, kind, forgiving, omnipresent, all-wise, al- knowing and all-powerful and can do anything for us. We can talk to Jesus and also to God.

Pastor Williams

Genesis starts out, "God is." So I don't think the human mind can consider God otherwise. God reveals Himself to us through the trinity. There are not three Gods, but one God. We see Him as the Creator of all life and that He gives us freedom to make choices. His justice, His righteousness...God is love and created us in His own image and particularly us, African Americans. We have to strive to live in His image as the Scripture teaches.

Pastor Boston

In the preaching experience, God is our Father, the creator and sustainer of us all. God is all-knowing, all-seeing, and is everywhere, in all parts of town as well as with my brother in Africa and India. At the same time, He can bring healing and wholeness in our lives.

3. Who is the Holy Spirit in the preaching experience?

Pastor Table

Out of the slavery experience, they knew that there was one who created them and wanted Him to become involved in their everyday life and living conditions. The same with the Holy Spirit in the preaching experience. He is not just someone who gives us goose bumps in a quavering and shaking experience. It is all right for us to shout, or dance, or celebrate in an ecstatic way, but in a Christian way. After all, what we have in God is something to be excited about, that over-powering expression as experiencing the Holy Spirit.

That is the very practical way the African-American preacher conveys to them that God is moving through them, "I feel my help coming," and people understand that terminology relates to the invisible God. They know that the Holy Spirit is present in their preaching, and their response is directly related to Him. He takes the people from the teaching aspect of the message to that which is celebrated. And the people respond by their expressions to the preaching experience. He becomes their lifter-upper and that is evidenced in their expression of excitement. He becomes their enlightener, their heavy load sharer. He becomes the Comforter because they begin to feel His presence and their burdens are lighter because of the conveyed experience in the black church.

Also, we look at the Israelites' experience in Egypt. So our way can be dark, therefore the Holy Scriptures become the light and the cloud of glory leads them, a pillar of fire by night, and the pillar of cloud by day. We look at Him as our way out, and follow His leadership because; we are committed fundamentally to the words of Jesus. So when He, the Holy Spirit, has come, He will lead you into the truth. So the teaching experience exposes the congregation to the fact that, yes, God is in heaven, Christ is in heaven, but the Holy Spirit is within you. And in that sense, you have the total presence of God, to get you out of your bondage as your Protector. So we have all this deliverance in the preaching experience.

Pastor Monroe

Needless to say, from the Pentecostal background, the great emphasis is the power of the Holy Spirit, the energizer, and the one that forces. We shall receive power after the Holy Spirit comes upon us.

Pastor Webb

I want them to know that the Holy Spirit is really the abiding presence of the Lord, meaning that He is present with us to help us in every situation, to teach us, to lead, and guide us. He is the one present in the absence of the physical Jesus. He walks with us, talks with us and, He is the one who applies the Word to our daily lives. In terms of our faith, faith calls into existence those things we cannot see, so in terms of the Holy Spirit, he helps us to do those things Jesus has commanded us to do. The Holy Spirit helps me to love the unlovable, to help those who despitefully use me, in this context to accomplish what God has planned for us to do. He is the abiding presence with me and in me. He is the Enabler.

Furlow: Question about God's revelation...How is God recognized?

I guess I deal with progressive revelation. We cannot comprehend all God is and what He wants us to know. We can never comprehend it at one time or in one setting and so God reveals it to us over time. I use the Bible, and how God reveals His plan to man over a span of time. Many years Jesus was concealed in the Old Testament, but in the New

Testament, Jesus was revealed, and God is still uncovering and revealing His plan to us. That's my understanding of that in terms of we live in the age of the Holy Spirit and God is revealing more things to us right now. We are in the last dispensation of the last age of the church and God has revealed to us over a period of time, unveiling, and uncovering.

Pastor Watson

Well, the Holy Spirit is the abiding presence of God, the absence of Jesus in the flesh. The Holy Spirit sustains us to do His holy will and to act out His will, His program; not seeing the Holy Spirit as just emotion, but feeling and believing that God is omnipresent.

Pastor Hayes

The Holy Spirit is the third person in the godhead. I teach that the Holy Spirit is a person with feelings, a comforter, a teacher, and guide. And whenever we need the Holy Spirit, He will come into our hearts and lives. I think with people they don't really understand, and it's mysterious and kind of a mystical happening in the church. He will come to live with us. He is the anointing of God's presence for us in our lives, and if we don't have the anointing in our lives as pastors and leaders, then we are just speaking words and emotions and not really preaching the proclamation of the gospel; just getting up and reading sermons and words.

So we as leaders and pastors must have the anointing of the Holy Spirit within us in order to have the presence of God living in us. And if the presence of God is living in us, then our sermons will be powerful, will motivate people, will change the lives of people, and they will feel the Holy Spirit in their presence. They will know the Holy Spirit. When they come into the service they will feel the presence. They might not fully understand what it is, but will know it is something different and it's the presence of the Holy Ghost.

Upon our baptism we receive the Holy Spirit into our hearts, but if we do not study God's Word, not praying and not living according to the laws of God, then the Holy Spirit is going to leave us. The Holy Spirit cannot live in an unclean place. So when that Holy Spirit leaves us, we have no covering, no protection, even through the blood may still cover us, and when we pray God will still answer, but we have no power, because the power is the Holy Spirit. That Holy Spirit comes and dwells in us. When we change and do what we want to do, then the Holy Spirit will leave us.

Pastor Williams

The Holy Spirit is God, the Holy Trinity. He inspires us and sometimes disturbs us to stir us up to incline us to reach our potential. He directs us, speaks to us in many different ways: through prayer, quietness, through other people, and all types of methods. The holy God is with us. He directs us to do God's will and to provide for us.

Pastor Mann

The Holy Spirit is in us and beside us. Wherever He is, He is within us. He empowers us to live our situations in life and to share our testimonies with those who are not in the body of Christ. He is a source to those who are in the body of Christ. I believe that the Spirit empowers us to comfort other believers in their time of trouble and encourage them with that which He has done for us and to us. This Holy Spirit works in a triad manner. He walks with us externally and also meets us and becomes more personal to each believer as He nurtures our mind to help us overcome. One of the wonderful things about the Holy Spirit is the responsibility of keeping our souls anchored in the Lord. Clay, Paul says that to the day of redemption, the soul is a transaction and we don't have to look to another because our salvation is in the Lord and a finished transaction. Because He paid it all for us.

Pastor Boston

The Holy Spirit is the unseen, but yet felt personality of the Godhead often described as the Holy Ghost that comes like the wind blowing, but one cannot always say from which direction the wind comes. We do know that we are refreshed when the Holy Ghost comes from whatever direction because we are helped in whatever condition we find ourselves.

4. How is your understanding of God made meaningful to your congregation?

Pastor Simms

I don't know how to answer that. Bible teaching, and how God has worked in my own life and experiences and the life of others. I think all of our preaching should point that out; what God has done in the life of someone, no matter what the text is. Someone can be given as an example to explain the text you're dealing with and in essence, all scriptures are meaningful. I ask people, did you hear the message? I say so what, and leave it for them to apply the sermon to their own lives, and sometimes they will tell me about it later on.

Pastor Monroe

I am always emphasizing the chapter about the prodigal son. No matter what we've done in life, no matter how far you have fallen, no matter how much you have messed up or the mistakes you've made, or how black your sins may be, you can make up your mind to come back to God and He will forgive and heal your soul.

May I back up for a moment just to go back to question three which ask about the Holy Spirit? You heard me mention that in our Pentecostal background, it is our belief that conversion is a mental part of the Holy Spirit and we are taught that there is a difference between being filled with the Spirit and baptized in the Spirit. So we move into what the old saints called the second blessing, we encourage people to come and receive the filling of the baptism. It's a sign of speaking in unknown tongues, so in our new members class we stress, now that you have accepted Jesus Christ, your sins have been washed away, you can get empowerment from the Spirit.

Pastor Watson

I see revelation as God's self-disclosure. He is always about disclosing Himself to us, in the ordinary common places in our world. He is revealing Himself and His will through events and circumstances, so it becomes the role of the preacher to point out to the church, where God is at work. Where God is active in some places where we would not necessarily see Him. How we see Him through the tragedy that just occurred. I see revelation as something that is constantly happening. The revelation of God and His Son is a one-time event, but beyond that He reveals Himself and it is our job to interpret what God is doing.

Pastor Hayes

I make God relevant to our people by letting them know that God is a very present help in times of trouble, He is there all the time whenever we need Him. He is present in our everyday lives and situations, even down to the minute things. I might want to buy something and I pray and say, God I can't find it, and the next thing I know, God directs me to find exactly what I'm looking for.

A case in point, I was speaking to a class last night about how God will be there for you. I had gone into a store to make a purchase. I saw a statue of Jesus on the counter and wanted to get it for our church but the cashier said it was not for sale. The manager had informed her that it was not for sale. However, I called for the manager who was out to lunch. So I waited for him to return. I prayed to God while I waited for him. I told the manager I wanted it for our church and he then gave it to me at no cost.

When we were on Master Street, we had planned to knock down the wall and extend the building. And we tried to fix up the church, but that was not God's plan for the Mt. Tabor Church. So God revealed to me that the foundation of the little church had to be relayed and then He would rebuild His church. I did not fully understand that, but a young lady shared with us in a Bible study that because the steward in charge of the Bible study took so long, I said, the time is far spent so we will have this Bible study next week. Then, the young lady said, "Why don't we let him talk as much as he wants to next week because he is the oldest member of the church and maybe he has a lot to say." I said to myself, he has taken up all the time now, but God was revealing Himself through this man taking up all the time talking about things in the past. But God laid it on the heart of that young lady to say that and the Spirit spoke to me and said, "Let's have an old members night and invite all the members to come back and talk about the past." So the following week I told them to bring other friends because my ministry was not growing. So the people came the following week. I get excited when I begin to tell this. They began to talk about things and I'll give you two points. One lady said they had raised money for choir robes and the pastor took the money to pay the assessment. In our church, if you don't pay, you will soon be gone.

Another lady said she had baked a cake for a dinner at the church and her cake was never served. The next Sunday she found the cake still there in the kitchen. And they said the cake was not good enough. So things like this cause strife in the church. So God had to reveal Himself, regarding the problem with the church. So I said the church needed an inner healing. Everybody lets get on our knees and let's pray. Forgive each other for the hurt and pain and animosity of the past and let's pray. We did and the church got on fire. People were crying and embracing each other and I realized then what God meant, that the church had to be relayed and rebuilt. He revealed that to me when I asked why the church was not growing.

Then Sunday morning when I went downstairs, the church was filled and has been ever since. What had to happen was, God had to reveal to me that I had to move myself out of the way because I came to this church believing that I had a little bit of experience, expertise, along with my husband. Because we were in leadership there, he was the superintendent of the Sunday School and I was over the Young Peoples' Department. We had done crusades and we came in with what we thought was expertise, but it didn't work there. What works in one church will not always work in another so you have to follow God's plan for the church. God will reveal to you what He will allow.

Now, suppose I did not listen to Him when He revealed to me that the foundation of this church had to be relayed. *"Upon the rock I build my church."* I cried and asked forgiveness and I went downstairs the next Sunday and the church was almost full and now the church is growing. All of this is related. So God reveals Himself even when we lose sight; God reveals Himself in many, many ways. When we didn't have money to do certain things, God revealed Himself. We had to do the roof at a cost of about $30,000. We were a small congregation, so God revealed to me how He was going to take care of it. We had a windstorm, knocked shingles off the roof, and according to the insurance company that's how we got that side of the roof fixed. We couldn't get this side fixed because the windstorm hit that side of the roof. That was early when we moved in here in 1988, and this happened about five years after we came here. But just here in June an emergency was declared by the President in Pennsylvania because of floods. The south side needed repairs, then again an act of nature, and God allowed this to happen and then the repair was completed. So God reveals Himself to us, we couldn't afford the work that needed to be done, but God revealed Himself through His acts of nature.

I believe God and not man or circumstances. So if I have a problem in this church, a physical or a problem with the congregation, I pray and trust God, I know He is coming, I don't know which way or when, but I tell others over and over that it was God who fixed this roof. So the work was just completed last week and it is more intricate than that. Never let the people forget. He brought us from 22nd and Master Street from a little church house to a cathedral. I try to preach sermons that people know about. Jesus used parables. I use things around us and things they/we are involved in, reminding them that it was God and not I.

Pastor Williams

As human beings we look at a small sector of life in terms of suffering.

Pastor Mann

I think God reveals himself and makes Himself visible in the lives of the faith community. Our faith is two-fold—the lives of those who believe in Jesus Christ and their lives of hope. You cannot distance God from hope as it relates to our faith. You cannot dismiss faith and not have hope. Once we dismiss hope, we have nothing to look forward to. We have everything to look forward to in the fullness of Jesus Christ. Once the spark of hope is ignited in a person's life, and he understands the source and cause of the reward we have, the hope enables him to look beyond his circumstances. This God can deliver, and we then do not have to remain in our sins and problems or self-pity.

Pastor Boston

God is involved, alive and well in our everyday living. He is performing His miracles, and I try to help people to not be so overwhelmed that they miss seeing God moving. Regardless of the seriousness or tragedy of a situation, if we look close enough and long enough we will see wholeness that God is able to impart.

God is good and has not forsaken us. God is moving and working on our behalf even when we know not or see not. That is one of the mysterious stages and personalities of God. He is always working on the behalf of His children even when we are being disobedient and going through difficult times when God is trying to move us to.

5. Which books of the Bible do you feel best address the conditions of the African-American church?

Pastor Simms

That's hard to say. In slavery times, liberation Exodus, Jews coming out of Israel, in Daniel the salvation theme and the fiery furnace, the lions den, I think those scriptures were used in the earlier years. Today, many ministers to get their point across about certain predictions especially use the Gospels—Matthew, Mark, and Luke. I think that might be a fault, too, in the African-American church.

In a sense, if you have the time as a pastor and can go from Genesis to Revelation throughout the years, you want a well balanced menu versus always from the gospels. Some ministers I know every Sunday, the text is taken from Matthew, Mark, and Luke or something from the Old Testament. The Bible is everything, a sword, a hammer, and a light. The pastor should be careful in looking over his records. It refers to what chapters in the Bible he has not preached, and those he has preached from a lot. The total picture of each kind of book, history, gospel, church letters, in my own I find myself going to the Letters and Psalms, I think is a personal devotion.

Pastor Monroe

I think you really have to look first at the book of Exodus. So much is said about the struggle and what race of people, as the African-American race struggles through the whole parts of lives, as we came out of Mother Africa, and their struggles. Joshua is another book, talks about conquest, the fight. If you're going to win you have to fight; you're not going to be sustained, or have it easy any more. I emphasize in my preaching that being African-American doesn't mean you are going to be better, but you have to fight all the way up. In addition, the books of Joshua and Psalms, we have the ability to rejoice and praise, no matter what we are suffering or experiencing. A song is quoted, "Satan may seem to gain, but there is a God who rules above and if we're right He will fight our battles."

Pastor Webb

I guess, in my preaching I probably have equal preference. The Old Testament intrigues me. It excites me in how I see Jesus and how the plan unfolds, but my teaching primarily comes from the New Testament because most of the teachings for the church are in the writings of Paul. So I teach from Paul's epistles, but I like to discover Jesus in the Old Testament; the types and symbols of the Old Testament. And one of my favorites is Genesis. The major themes are in Genesis. In my study of Genesis a few years ago I saw Jesus and Calvary in Genesis, but the church was developed in the New Testament.

Pastor Watson

Conscientiously, I don't have a preference, but I think I seen to gravitate toward the New Testament because of the life of Jesus and the history of the church. I think that lecturers want to be faithful to the whole Bible, but I probably, preach more from the New Testament. But I am aware of that and try to straighten that out, but always under the unction of the Holy Spirit. The Holy Spirit is not concerned about which books I preach from, but that the entire Bible is preached.

Pastor Hayes

I don't think that there are any special books. I believe that the Bible as a whole, if you know how to relate certain instances, the past, the present, then you can show the people, God in the past and the present. And you can relate it to African Americans and anybody else. It is up to the preacher to pull it together and show the people how to present it and show the people how it works. I don't preach only from the gospels and I know there are certain books, but you can relate the African-American experiences to almost all the books.

Pastor Williams

One thing I like to emphasize is that we as humans have a tendency and seem to look at small sections of life, especially in terms of suffering and in terms of life and that God is not just. They tend not to see the blessings and how far God has taken us as a people. We see the beauty and strength of God and His guidance, and then it is no way possible to think that God is unjust. Without the presence of God, whenever I preach I try to emphasize that no matter what the situation is today, you have already seen the tremendous blessings of God. Sometimes I feel in conflict with some of my white brothers and sisters, when they talk about the past and how good things were in the past, and how moral and religious people were in the past. But based on my own history and experiences, I saw a time when my grandmother told stories of how they came through bad times, and only through the grace of God to inspire people. I try to make the people aware that God was always there through our history as a testimony, and who God is and that God is present today, remembering the resurrection and eternal life and His Kingdom after death and in the life as well. As long as we are on God's side, we can rest with assurance that God is going to be there. There is no doubt in my mind and He has given us freedom of choice. But the biggest thing is that God loves us and gave His life for us so we have a responsibility to love people and we should not seek revenge, but seek justice. When people mistreat us, we must be careful how we react in seeking justice.

I frequently refer to the Old Testament Genesis, especially. We are created in God's image. I emphasize God's promise to Abraham as the father to all people and creations. We are not a separate people that out of His promise, we see the struggles, even to the chosen ones, and to all human beings there is always a constant struggle, but God is there to see us through. So it is important to see that and also in Genesis things can be turned around. In the story of Joseph how man can plan something for your detriment, but God is able to use bad for something good. I see, to my way of thinking, advancements come through wartime. I believe that because people find themselves in situations and begin to realize who God is and He is able to take a bad situation and make something good out of it. So the book of Genesis in the Old Testament and Luke in the New Testament. And the book of Hebrews addresses the historical walk and the book of James.

Pastor Mann

I don't know if there is a book that I feel more comfortable in addressing African-American conditions. I feel that the Bible needs to be preached in its wholeness—the Old Testament and the New Testament. The Old Testament parallels the African-American experience based upon the similar experiences of the children of Israel. Yet, it reveals when a nation or a race of people has chosen to turn their back on the living God, there is a wrath of God on the nation or person. It has to be experienced; the New Testament and Old Testament warn us of the sinfulness of the world, but the hope God gives us rests in Him.

Pastor Boston

Certainly, in the African-American church, we have seen many parallels of our plight and those of the children of Israel. Numbers, Leviticus, Isaiah are books that show similar conditions and struggles. We also see parallels in the New Testament, in Paul's letters, Revelation, and Acts.

6. What connections, if any, do you see existing between the life issues that members of your congregation face and the kind of songs that are sung in the preaching context?

Pastor Simms

Someone has accused African-American churches, and it has been said that songs are personal. I and me and what God has done for me, what I am doing—songs of that nature and that praise Him and what He did for me. When I was down and out He picked me up. I talked to Him last night. I walk with God—songs of that nature. Some say many of the spirituals are very personal. My argument is that so are the Psalms. When you read the book of Psalms, you see life issues.

I do use hymns quite a bit in my preaching. I have about fifteen hymnals here, only thing is that when you quote poetry/hymns it slows you up in your preaching, so I may not use it at the end of my sermon.

We should not forget our spirituals and should hold on to them, "It's me, it's me, Oh Lord, standing in the need of Prayer." I hope we don't forget the good words, some of the stuff we hear now is, what you would think you would hear in a night club and so repetitious, as if God is hard of hearing. That bothers me to hear before preaching, even when the preacher preaches and a guy is playing music while he is preaching. You don't really need that. The Holy Spirit doesn't need that either.

I'm not sure how to relate what we sing to the preached word. One of the answers is to look at the cycle of history. If you look at those hymn books, you find that most of that stuff was written in the late 1800 to early 1900, and here is this wave, this cycle of missions, of music, of styles of preaching, all of which is up to the Lord to do what He wants. It's in God's hands, and I think, if someone teaches the truth, then I should accept the truth as the Holy Sprit leads me regardless of whether a white man or a European said it.

One of my criticisms of the guys who talk so much about Euro-centralism, with all their education and degrees, they also spout a lot about names of Europeans to back up the theology and what they were taught about in seminary. To me this is contradictory as for black music and the gospel we do have ...C. A. Tindley...you might like the words, but the style is...I don't know how to put that, so much of the gospel music is not scriptural and the emotional content bothers me. No melody just a beat and that's about it. So talking about Euro-centric or Afro-centric does not bother me if physically, it has a nice melody to it. It is subjective. I find no fault to it. We do have some blacks—Dorsey, Tindley and some newer fellows—who have done some good stuff and I enjoy it, but I never thought too much about it. I think more about when it comes to theology versus Afro-centric, but I can understand the criticism.

Pastor Monroe

We are taking on a theme song, "More Than Enough." Jehovah is more than enough to provide for every need and heal every sickness. He is more than enough.

Pastor Webb

For awhile, there was not a whole lot of connection for this generation because the songs connected when I was growing up. But here more recently I've learned to connect with the songs being sung today to get them to where I want them to go. There is a song we use to sing, "A charge to keep I have and a God to glorify, to serve this present age, my calling to fulfill." And so I feel that I'm called to serve this present age. So I have to connect with them where they are in order to take them to where I think God is leading them, and so they sing contemporary songs today.

I see a stronger connection in order for my preaching to be relevant to take them to the next level. So I've learned to connect with them because for a long while I was still using the songs I grew up with and I tell folks that I love the gospels, but I've learned to tolerate contemporary music and the kind of stuff they're singing. The songs tell a people's story. During slavery it was our spirituals. When you listen to the spirituals you hear songs like, "Everybody talking 'bout heaven ain't going there" that carry a certain message. "I got shoes, you got shoes, all of God's children got shoes." That sends a message. They could envision the future. With the gospels, you get a more jubilant song, e.g., "My Soul looks back and wonder, how I got over." "Oh, happy day!" That's good news! That's the gospel message.

Now we're in another era. We're in a mixed era—the gospel and contemporary music—which sends a mixed signal. I don't know whether you want to shout or dance, and you look at this generation and they act so confused from the messages of the songs. It will work in the church or in the club. That's how we get that cross over stuff, but we have to connect with those folks and teach the gospel now or we might never be able to connect.

Pastor Williams

That's one of the areas, serving in an integrated church that has been a struggle. I already have the song chosen that I want at my funeral. It's "Going Up Yonder." But I know I have a responsibility to the whites in the congregation to teach about racism, about the conditions of people and being true Christians. I try to do it in a way so as not to show anger.

Pastor Boston

We are a worshiping congregation, even in this new millennium. Life is not a bowl of cherries. So we are compelled to sing songs of joy and lively spirited songs to usher us into an atmosphere to worship God in spirit and truth. So all that we sing—anthems, hymns or gospels—are sung to feed our souls to set the proper context for the Word of God.

7. To what extent do earlier African-American preachers influence how and what you preach today?

Pastor Simms

As I look back over the men I've heard over the years, most of them developed their sermons rather well, although

Christ wasn't always central. Whatever the text was and their ability to tell the story or illustrate, I was amazed and it was very helpful. Stuff that I read earlier, sixteenth and seventeenth centuries was very long. It was so complicated to read, I wondered what it was like to listen as it was preached one hour and longer. But early African-American preachers have influenced me in how and what I preach today. I admired them and their auditory. I wish I had that gift of gab. And very often they have inspired me to do better as far as delivery is concerned. I have a problem there, so most of my preaching is from manuscript, I read my manuscript over and over again, ten times, in order to have some eye-to-eye contact without it. But listening to those men and the different styles and approaches and the way they worked their sermons out has been very helpful to me over the years.

As for what I preach, well, because of Dr. Powell's influence, whenever he took a text, he developed it and dealt with the context—for whom it was written and what it meant to the people at that time.

Pastor Monroe

Well, this is a very touching time; I remember my childhood days in the church. We always talked about, by and by and when we cross over Jordan, what God has in store for us. That's what the pastors I served under as a child taught us, but I'm a great believer that the God that I serve is a right now God; He has blessings in store. My favorite scripture is John Chapter 10. There is a great emphasis that I put on abundant living right now. Being a Christian, we should have a high quality of life, not that of a second class citizen.

Pastor Webb:

I came out of a culture of an oral tradition, and some of the older preachers were very colorful with words and so I see it as painting pictures with words. You could not help but see what they were talking about; they would describe it with such validity, describing the coming of Jesus Christ and the Second Coming as if on a chariot. I came out of a tradition where the people did not think the preacher was really preaching if he used a manuscript for over half of his sermon. At some point he had to close the Bible and get away from his script. Folks looked at him as a person keeping things very simple. They used verses that were not confusing or too complicated. And that's how earlier preachers influenced my preaching. I heard Dr. Gardner Taylor say as he talked about the Garden of Eden and Calvary, and of life over in Revelation so vividly that you had to see what he was talking about because he painted the picture with words. Guys like the late James H. Jackson, who was another master of painting pictures with words, and Samuel Ray. Those guys intrigued me.

Pastor Watson

I think we all as preachers stand in a tradition, not just an African-American tradition, but in a larger tradition to an earlier period of the fathers; and the Old Testament prophets of a long tradition which should affect our preaching. So when we stand in the pulpit, we ought to embrace, but not hinder us from developing styles of communication in the age in which we preach. Those who preached for one hour or more, and that was the norm, but we live in a different world today. In many of our churches today, if the sermon lasts more than an hour, the effectiveness may take a half of an hour. So the people who preached affect us and especially by the preachers we grew up with and admired. So they served as models, preachers from our childhood and early years as development. We look at them and say our preaching styles are affected by how we put our sermons together. I have my own. My father was my primary teacher, and he is still living as a retired pastor. I think I'm a little bit like him.

Pastor Hayes

When I think back, years ago, listening to the preachers then, I did not always understand, and that was natural, because I was young. But there was one thing that stayed with me all of my life: what they taught me about Jesus. He would always be there and by putting my faith in Jesus Christ and believing that He would help you. I believed in what they told me. God gave me the gift of faith when I was eleven years old. It shaped who I am and the reason I have this kind of faith is because the preaching and teaching I received in the Sunday school and the preaching, because it was together. I was taught that nothing was too hard for God and that if I called on Jesus that God was going to answer. His Son allows me to receive that which I asked for. So when I was eleven years old and living down south I was riding my bicycle and another kid ran into me. I fell and this finger was cut so that it was only hanging by the skin. My dad came and took me to the hospital. Well, I heard the doctor telling my Dad that they were going to amputate from the joint. And I began to pray and believe God. My preacher had preached about and said He could do miracles, so I wrapped my hand in that towel and ran off the bed and down the hall. When they caught me I looked up in my fathers eyes and said,"Have mercy Jesus. If they would just sew it then it would knit back together." The doctor said no, because gangrene might set in and you could lose your whole hand. I said to my dad, "In the name of Jesus, please don't let them cut my finger off."

So my father looked at them and said because she believes, I'll take the responsibility. The doctor said; you will have to bring her back every day to change the bandages and watch it, so dad said,"Okay." That's when God gave me the gift of faith, when I was a kid. It was because I believed those ministers. It helped me to be what I am today. I'm a person of great faith. I don't believe man or circumstances, I believe God. Even when we got this building, our Bishop said, "We don't have $58,000 to lend you to get that church. Where do you think we will get that kind of money?" I said, "God will make a way." He said, "God will surely have to make the way." I believe God, and those parables in the Bible. I knew that Jesus did them, and I believe He will do them for me.

Also, I was dying when I was thirteen years old. I had lock jaw, and in the South, you know how it was. My body locked, and my jaws locked. I had an out of body experience. I found myself soaring up to heaven, and I wanted to die to be at peace with God by praying consciously and unconsciously that God would heal me in order to live for others and they would know about the goodness of God. God allowed me to see the whole picture of life in a nutshell. I did not understand the commitment I had made. I meant it, but I had to grow to understand what I had asked and said. Out of all of my family and friends, I was the one who loved to be in church, and listen to the old people sing those hymns. I was never bored; I loved it. It just sunk into my spirit and my sister and one brother are back in the church now, but the others just go when they feel like it, not really committed.

Pastor Mann

Earlier African-American preachers and pastors helped me in the sense that all preaching that is taken seriously and the eternal truths go back to God. And all of that is the Word of God in the Word of God. Those are the truths that are maintained in the Word.

Pastor Boston

In many respects, I see earlier African-American preachers as having some of the same challenges we are faced with today. General themes, but more of it in regards to what we have to deal with today and maybe less but more over topics of today. Henry Nichols, pastor of this congregation for thirty-nine years, Charles Albert Tinley, and Ben Smith of Deliverance Church started with ten members and grew to ten thousand at one point. People were dedicated, trusted, and relied on God and out of doing the will of God. They were given the will of God and dealt with the needs of the people. So it's out of living with God and His people, the two at best bring you to the point of that preaching moment.

8. How is God and Jesus Christ preached where the African-American male is concerned?

Pastor Simms

I know what I would like to say is that preaching that God in Christ for the African-American Christian man to be a leader in his family, to know Christ, to be saved, but knowing our background, knowing how mixed up and messed up it is, fatherless homes and families, and so much depending on the women and mothers and especially grandmas, we had a saying, thank God for grandmothers. But there is a need and some churches have hammered away at this black male thing and the need for Christ and therefore to strengthen the family and the church. I talk about this quite often and the need for male leadership in our churches, and their responsibilities. There is a Bible basis for it; God made man, and put man in charge. So how is Jesus Christ preached? I need to give that a little more thought.

Pastor Monroe

Realizing that most of our churches are filled with women and children, one species that is most difficult to catch is the African-American male. So in this church the attempt is to bring to the conscience of the male that we were God's first creation. The Bible teaches that in Genesis, the woman came after us and was taken from the male. God made man first, and gave him authority over all. So God gives man a great responsibility as head of his house, head of this family, and the children.

So the church plays the minor part because we see his children one hour in Sunday school, two to three hours for worship, but that child is his twenty-four seven per week. So he must become the leader, teacher of his own household. If his family is to know his God, then they are not going to know God through the pastor but through his teaching, his training, and his example. They have to see him reading the Bible, see him praying daily, and leading them to the worship experience. Surely, God depends on him.

In fact I will bring back to his remembrance that although Eve partook of the fruit first and gave it to Adam, God did not question Eve first. God questioned Adam. Adam had the major responsibilities. I put great emphasis on you. Your family goes as you go. That joy of your household and spirit of your household, depends on you.

Furlow: Do you have a male ministry?

Yes, we have men's fellowship and meet one day per month, a mid-week service. We also do a lot on Saturday through various boards and meetings. But our greatest thing is the men's conference we have each year, having notable preachers, and have workshops. We have a men's breakfast with 900 to 1,000 men for breakfast.

I remember when I founded this church of members with eighteen children. My first members were a hand-full of women, but I had a consecration service and since then, a large part of the church is men. I guess the leadership of this church is in the hands of men. Men have to be seen leading in the church. People say that most men minds see only women and children in the church, but it's hard to come to Mt. Airy and not be stunned by the fact that men are doing so much for this. On Men's Day you will see a hundred fifty men in the choir. So if other men walk in the front door and see them singing and the officers and ushers are men. That's impressive!

Pastor Webb

Yes, and I've discovered that Islamic/Muslim teachings for the African-American male, not wanting to accept and see Jesus as less than Lord. I said earlier that I teach Jesus as Lord of Lords. I don't leave Him as a babe in a manger in Bethlehem neither as still on the cross, but I present Him as a bold, voracious Savior and not a wimp. That's what the brothers want to hear. I show in the Scriptures, if you think He is weak, look at Him in the temple as He chases the money changers; look at Him when everybody is running yelling leprosy. Jesus does not flinch. All He said was "Be clean" and you were cleansed. He is not a weak Savior. Even at His weakest, He is stronger than anything we know about. The weakest of God is stronger than man and He is wiser than man who cuts across the grain. Jesus did not go along with the tradition. The Pharisees and Sadducees were always fighting and bickering, but Jesus was a bold Savior and elder brother. A lot of that weakness comes from the white man's religion, which has an Islamic/Muslim slant, that's how they present Jesus when they want to present their doctrines. Jesus is bold and voracious.

Pastor Watson

I try to preach to the needs of people, rather male or female, unless I'm asked to address men, for Men's Day or a male breakfast, or something like that. I try to address issues that concern them, but I don't set out to just preach to men. I try to recognize that my congregation is made up of both men and women and to help older people. And I try to preach a sermon that includes all, not excluding one group or another. That is not to say that I'm not aware of some of the special issues, but I think a more effective way of looking at that is to look at the church itself and see what it is about the church that does not attract men. We basically feminize the church and we appeal to women because they are in the majority. But what is it in the church that men want to be involved in? Like having men's ministries and having those kinds of formats. I still want to preach a sermon that will aid in the transformation of lives regardless of sex.

I think sometimes we, as preachers, play into the fact that of the women we have in our churches and criticizing why men are not coming to church rather than seeing why they are not going. Make a concerted effort in finding out. There's something about the socialization of girls and boys. We raise girls and boys differently. Boys believe they shouldn't cry, or show any kind of emotion. They ought to be self-sufficient in order to be somebody. No wonder they have the inability to express themselves. To say to a woman "I love you" and the feeling of going to church is a sign of weakness.

So we have to look at a lot of things. Preaching is just one aspect and not the only issue. I would hope that if I preached a sermon, how to be a Christian man, I hope that I also talk about a Christian for everybody, unless I'm doing a breakfast for men only, then that's a different arena.

Pastor Hayes

That's the most difficult I have encountered as a pastor, trying to get black men into the church. Not so much the difference I preach in my preaching ministry, but what we have done is focus on our blackness through teaching. In our Bible institute, we've taught about the first man who was a black man that was created. We teach things over and over again. That brought about a lot of interest and men came out and studied about who they were as the first man and it made them feel good about themselves.

I do realize that we need to do some things in this area, and I think even more than the preaching they need the teaching and nurturing. As I said early on, so many of our families now are single mothers only and so our men have a difficult problem with God and the Holy Spirit and all male images. And it is because of the mother and grandmothers being the matriarchs and always being there doing for them. I think this has caused a problem with a lot of our men becoming homosexuals because they are identifying with their mothers rather than their fathers. So this is an area I am focusing on.

We have men's ministry and my husband works with them and other male members of the congregation, and our male minister associate. It is most difficult to get the men to come in and take God's plan. It's going to take a lot of preaching, teaching, and praying because our black men are really hurting. We know that some of the problems come from slavery and the urban setting where black men are not given jobs. Jobs are given to black women before they are given to black men. I believe black men want to be good fathers and bread winners as your father and my father were taught; just as most of us who came from the South. We were taught to respect our fathers first and everything now is pointing to the men and putting them down. Even in the church, pastors saying, we aren't looking for the men to do as well as the women because it is not as many men and there are women and things like that are not lifting the men up. Look at the congregation, we only have a few men here. We always have more women. Well, we know that is true, that's a given so we need not say it, but to praise and congratulate them and give them things to do. Let them work.

We give the young men a few nickels just to have them around the church and give them something to do. They could be out in the streets so give them a little something to help with the cleaning. We cannot afford to pay them, but we give them a little something to encourage them. We wrap our arms around them, teach them their roots and how they are to be proud of who they are, and I think that will help in the future

Have them sit up front and not have them scattered. Encourage, praise, and show appreciation. Lift them up, stop beating them up, and stop bashing them from all elements of society. Teach them to believe that if they trust God everything will be all right.

Pastor Mann

I think I would approach that a little differently. I think the African-American males have to be reached through preaching and also through demonstrated life. It has to be demonstrated through a way that I can gain his confidence and trust in me. The preaching aspect more readily received and the pastor enters into fellowship with the African-American male that gives him the comfort and the willingness to trust the preaching experience. If I live my life in a demonstrated way then I get respect; therefore, it disarms the suspicion of the quote, unquote black preacher. It opens his mind and heart to my preaching and teaching to establish his trust level. And then he tells other men to come see and listen and hear the teaching. Once you are able to teach biblical truths, then it will become relevant to African-American men. But I must hasten to say that I do not believe that the principle of the gospel should be lowered to others' standards. The God we serve is still able to transform minds.

Pastor Boston

We still hold that from the beginning, as far as the Bible is concerned, the man is the provider, the protector of the family. And this is still true. We sometimes find ourselves in the women's movement as well as Affirmative Action, but we still hold that God set man as the head of the household. In January, we celebrated "Men in the House," which alluded to the Psalmist, that we are made a little lower than angels are and God has given us dominion.

We cannot avoid our responsibilities, although many men have not gotten themselves into a position to care for a wife and family or to be rooted and grounded in the faith. That was one of the things lifted up in the Men's Day program. Ben Smith lived the life as an example.

9. How does the history of African Americans in this country inform the content of your preaching today?

Pastor Simms

What we have gone through about black slavery in this country! I am very much concerned that blacks begin to know, in a better way, Jesus Christ and what the Bible teaches, and live the kind of lives that will please the Lord. Looking back at life during slave days, in some states and counties where it was illegal, black people could not be taught how to read or write. And blacks listening to the preaching of the whites and taking it as the Holy Spirit led, learned how to develop in their own way and style.

I realize that and because of their lack of training, much of our preaching has not been as doctrinal as I would like, personally. We must have doctrinal teaching in order to have a goal, something to shoot at. Doctrine is the basis and application. If we jump into application and have no doctrine, there is the danger of Semitism, ignorance, emotionalism, and stuff like that. So I think we have a better balance now than we had fifty or sixty years ago. This may also be a cause for some of the cults. Some of the cults are due to a lack of doctrine and also economics. The history of African Americans in this country informs the content of your preaching today, very much so; black slavery and the Bible, things of that nature.

Pastor Monroe

Well, a study in history is filled with great heroes of the past. Sorry to say that in my generation we've done nothing. Every invention was made by the whites, but I think when you make an in-depth search, you'll find that we've made a major part in the formation of this country. If you don't have knowledge of your history, you don't have an appreciation of your presence or future. History brings out pride. The word *pride*— we need to be proud of who we are, of our forefathers, pride of the fact we're a part of the African race; not really knocking the other races, but being pride of who you are.

Pastor Webb

To a great extent, particularly in deliverance as God being a deliverer who overrides any situation. Again I think it was God who delivered us out of slavery just as He delivered the children out of bondage and Egypt. I don't believe in the loving white folks or the smart black folks, I believe it was the hand of God. So that history involves our preaching and I can show folks that He delivers and is working in our favor. When

I look at the book of Esther, even though God's name is not mentioned, it does not mean that God is not at work. So you may not be able to see Him immediately in your situation, but that does not mean that He is not working in your behalf. In the salvation story, He delivers.

Pastor Watson

Preaching to the African-American church is obviously steeped in tradition because of our oppression. In my preaching, I'm always aware of such things as deliverance and inclusion because I think we identify with the people in the Bible who were oppressed, outcast, and rejected by the larger society. So those things are very important for us, particularly the social justice messages. Some of the TV teaching preaching, there is on prophetic preaching, or about social justice issues. I think every sermon should deal with God's love for us, His care, how He delivers us, and the issue of hope and concern. Preach out of our own cultural context and recognize that the gospel is greater than our scope.

Pastor Hayes

I often preach sermons and refer back to our heritage as black people and where God has brought us. And I let the people know that God has been with us even from the African continent and even on the slave ships where only the strong survived. I let them know that it was a part of God's plan to bring us from Africa to this country in order to help build this nation, this country. We are a part of the fabric, so nothing can be said or done to take away our contribution to this society and this country. This recent incident has touched the people to where they should have been so many years ago. Through so many other wars, when our men came back from fighting, they still treated us as second class citizens. They kept jobs from us and did all those other things, housing etc. Our country should have treated all people alike. So I think that God had to do something to strike their their love ones, their homes, and their economy. That hurts! Now, they're saying, "God, Bless America" and they're not looking at color anymore. Black or white, they're all talking and smiling and I hope and pray that this will continue. Yes, "God bless America," but we cannot forget where we came from—Africa.

I'm proud of my heritage. I went to Africa in 1996, and I often wondered...I'm a very emotional person. I love people and I love God and being emotional you show love. God showed His love through His Son, Jesus Christ, so when I placed my feet on the African shores a part of me that was missing came together.

I love God and people. I praise God and dance to the Spirit. I'm just an African by birth. I believe in my roots and my heritage. Sometimes I have been criticized because a few of our congregation members are Puerto Ricans, but I am who I am and I am proud of whom I am. My father is a Philippine and my mother is black, and I never think of myself as being part this or that. Members of my family don't want to be black, and I've gotten on them about that. I'm proud of my Africa so I share it. We are so blessed and creative as a people. I thank You, Jesus. I thank You, Jesus. I thank You, Jesus. I thank you, Lord, for you brought me from a mighty long ways.

Pastor Horton

Well, the thing about it is, I have not been able to run across any one book that states what went on in the African-American churches and their inception. I've read books that said the history of the oldest church is down in South Carolina, established in seventeen something. You get matches to that with the Vine Baptist Church and the First Baptist Church in Petersburg, Virginia back in 1775, in Williamsburg, Virginia back in 1770s and the First African Church here in Philadelphia. St. Thomas Episcopal is over two hundred years of age, and Zoar, which was an underground railroad. When you look back and see one of our churches is one hundred years old, that's old.

There is a Catholic church a few years ago that was one hundred seventy-five years old, but you don't run across a lot in the northern cities. There are more southern churches that are really old. Our church, First Baptist of Berwyn is over one hundred years old. Ninth Street church is an old church. New Bethel in Philadelphia is quite old also. Mt. Carmel, White Rock, and Monumental are about one hundred seventy-five years old. Union Baptist and Shiloh are above one hundred fifty years. Tindley Temple is old, but they changed their name when they moved to South Broad Street. United Methodist belongs to the Delaware Conference from Virginia to New York City with all black churches. Now they have a Philadelphia conference.

Pastor Mann

How we preach is often dictated by our experience. Our life experience cannot be divorced from life and that becomes who we are and as we see the grace of God working through and in us. That becomes the basis. Those experiences are communicated to the people to show them the relevancy of God's grace. So I don't believe we can preach the gospel of Jesus Christ void of our experiences. Personal experience with God in Jesus Christ and the divinity is coupled with my human and personal experience, and thus cannot be void of who we are. Jesus Christ would have us to be sincere about who we are in Christ Jesus. The historical aspect is that God is. He is able to bring us out of our situations and circumstance just as our forefathers did during slavery. The unmistakable hand of God freed men as a result of being in Christ Jesus.

Pastor Boston

I see from reading about African-American history, heroes, heroines, gifts, and the talents of those before us it helps us rise up against different circumstances. Our history is not a life of riches and convenience; rather, it was a life of struggles and hard work and sacrifices. The Scriptures undergird the fact of being ambassadors of peace and fighters for righteousness and justice.

10. How do you preach about justification and sanctification in the midst of oppressive social, economic, political and religious systems?

Pastor Simms

I have been accused of not dealing with the whole man. I may have said to you before if I have a splinter in my little finger, my whole man hurts. So I think that God has called me to preach the Bible, to preach principles, and what we learn about Him, and then we take that knowledge into society, on their jobs, in their homes. The other idea might be that we have it both ways, a church with a credit union, bowling team, Boy and Girl Scouts, and health clinics. That's one idea, but I like the other way. I really prefer that you come to church and hear the inspired Word of God, live a clean life in such a terrible oppressive, social, religious, political, economic living system. I prefer that because I think that is more of a challenge. Some would say that it does not give us the clout we should have as Christians; it's too individualistic. I preach against social evils, economic evils and totality including racism, and all the junk that goes on. I am writing my own biography now.

Seventy-five letters have been printed across the country, taking white people to task because of hypocrisy. Some guys do not know this, and say that I have been brained washed as if I do not have the Holy Spirit on my own. All three churches that I've pastored had white members and my last pastorate, Faith Fellowship Baptist Church, had two white ladies married to black men. So I do not stand up in the pulpit and blast whites in that sense, but I talk about evil in the Bible and in my writings they know where I stand. I mention the subject too, but in my preaching I don't. My emphasis is that getting the Christian inside straightened out so he can live in all kinds of oppression. Some will say that's too passive, that we should not just preach it, but go out and march, to vote. I encourage them to vote, but not how to vote. So as I look at my preaching and sanctification and justification, it's been what I call to get you to be a cool cat Christian no matter what your environment. Are you the Christian man/woman on the inside, and can you stomach all the junk that can happen to you on the outside? My philosophy is that things will get worst going down hill, but do all I can to help others, knowing that what ever I do, its still going down hill. I think it's realistic, and I preach along these lines. Strong on the inside, stuff will not take away your joy of salvation.

Pastor Monroe

Let me approach this from this perspective. It is believed and taught that the Jews are God's chosen. Starting with the line of Abraham, Jesus Christ comes through that line. And there is a great emphasis on His being special as far as God is concerned. Yet, I think that if you look at the life of His chosen, you have to admit that there was a lot of oppression.

I believe that in His understanding that the best comes out of a person when we go through. You never know how to lead until you first learn how to follow. You can never be the head until you know what it is to be the servant My understanding about the forty years in the wilderness has always been a struggle for me. Coming out of Egypt and eleven days away, and yet this prepared them to conquer the Promised Land. Maybe they would not have had the strength or faith to endure the toughness of the experience. So that experience made them ready for the conquering of the land.

I really do believe, and please don't take this as being narrow on my part, but I believe the eyes of the church, the black church, and I believe that God is getting us prepared. The struggle we're going through and have gone through because He knows that before He comes back that we will be key leaders. Whatever is going on in the religious churches today, the day will come when we will have major leadership positions. When you talk about the motherland, only the strongest survived and the weak died. We will float to the top if given the chance. So I am not totally disturbed because I know God is there. About fifteen years ago, I was on the board with Oral Roberts, and he said it would only be a matter of time.

Pastor Webb

We are a people of faith and we have to live by God's standards and believe even though we can't see the end that God is looking out for our best interest, and some how, some way God will work it out. Justification is a part of God's standards, so we are finite creatures, and we cannot understand everything God has in store for us. If we did, then God would not be God. I do not understand how God makes a brown cow that eats green grass and produces white milk. I do not understand that, but it does not mean that it doesn't happen; or even how my body systems work together, brain to arm and sends impulses, etc. So I accept these things by faith because I can't see the total picture right now. It is like being in church: one group will ask you to do something, but I have to look at the bigger picture.

Pastor Watson

Well, God is just. I preach it in a way that God is a just God and expects obedience from us and if not there are consequences. If we don't do the right thing then, there are consequences that affect us. At the same time, in preaching God's justice, we ought to preach His mercy so that one will never come out of listening to a sermon about justice and not sense that God is also a God of love and mercy and gives us a balance.

Pastor Hayes

I preach that God is a just God and sometimes we just don't understand. Because God is just, we can know that whatever God does or allows, the reason is to bring us closer to Him and to where He is trying to bring us. No man can stand just before God. When God sees the blood of Jesus covering us, He hears our prayers and supplications and He looks down on us as righteous. Whatever He does, He does well and whatever He allows, He allows.

Pastor Horton

I would say that the state the people were in made it seem as though their implicit faith in God was their only source of help. But once they got their liberation, they still found out that they needed God, their one source of power, comfort, and everything else. America is a kind of capitalistic society. As it is, blacks really did not count. But the more black people move up the ladder, became more overweight, more educated...but back there the church was their means for a better life. And whites went down South and started schools for blacks. Such schools included Virginia Union, St. Paul, and schools in Georgia, such as Morehouse and Spelman in Atlanta, and others. As far as blacks are concerned, blacks are still using the church to reach certain goals. But sometimes I don't know if there is a lot of spirituality. Take for example Clayton in NY. When you analyze Clayton, he was in a community of blocks and blocks of people. I understand that he could get up on a Sunday morning and say I need this or that and he got it. Just from middle class folks with nice jobs and nice homes. You cannot find that everywhere in America. Fighting for these political and economic positions in our churches creates a danger. I think there is a tendency to trust in political and economic positions more than spirituality. I think a lot of our younger ministers have that in mind and all that money out there.

Justification and sanctification in the midst of an oppressive social, economic, political and religious systems: God is just, but you ask people of color, and most of them will say He is on the side of the rich and powerful. When you look at the justice of God, you look at where we came from and where we are now. I feel like this: the providence of God brought us to where we are now. By all sense of where we came from and where we are now, how in the world did we get there? Look at what is happening now. Yes, Clarence Thomas is on the Supreme Court, but we feel that it was because a white president put him there. The Negroes did not want him. So how do we account for two girls, Venus and Serena, now being millionaires? Tennis was not a sport for blacks, but now look where we are. Althea Gibson and Arthur Ashe. Now, they have things named after them. How would whites explain that? *The Inquirer* does not give the girls a lot of coverage, but *The New York Times* does. There is an Italian girl trying to beat the girls and they are trying to rate her as number two, but Serena said she does not care because she has the eight hundred and fifty thousand dollars to prove she is number two. So things are designed somehow to keep us down, but black folks keep on coming up. Hank Aaron broke the home run record in baseball. So they grudgingly give him praise and they look to find a loophole, but we achieve in spite of it. So, I'm a great believer in the divine power and that God moves, or else how would we be in the places we are in now. God is all holy and powerful. Look at West Point and Annapolis once closed to African Americans, but now we got there. Blacks are admirals and generals. My own daughter has such a ranking. She does not like for me to talk about it, but look where she is! God works in mysterious ways.

Pastor Mann

The justice of God and the condition of people may be seen when God permits bad things to happen to good people. It does not mean that God is not a just God. He remains just because those of us in Jesus Christ know that in God, things work together for the good of those in Jesus Christ. For something we have scriptural support.

Dr. Furlow, one of the things I try to hammer home to the people is that, God is consistently who He is no matter what happens in our personal, church, or family lives. The circumstance never changes God. He is consistently God. Always, He is good and a just God regardless of what I go through in life. *"And I am with you, even unto the end of the world."* He is with me and in me and I can bear whatever He brings or me my selfishness brings on me or leads me to a misfortune. He never deviates from who or what He is.

Pastor Boston

I have come to understand the fight against principalities. Our fight is twenty-four hours, seven days a week; never a time to rest, no time for vacation. There is always some system—social or political—where we have to raise our voices for justice. Evil runs rampant in our homes, on the street, on the job or wherever. We have to take a stand. Are we going to only wave the palms or be cross bearers? We just cannot stand in the crowd waving and cheering. We must be willing to go the last mile of the way, even speaking out and being in harm's way, if necessary, for justice.

11. *Do you tend to preach more from the Old or New Testament, and why?*

Pastor Simms

I'm not very strong in Hebrew language, yet I like the Psalms and what I get out of them. Most of my Old Testament preaching is from the book of Psalms. On the other hand, I love to preach the church letters to the saints in Philadelphia. I try to balance it out through Revelation. However, I bend over backwards, maybe too much, in preaching Matthew, Mark, Luke and John because I hear so many other black preachers using the Gospels on the radio and at the conference. I believe that the letters to the churches is what the church today needs. And as they are written, you can't avoid picking something up from the Old Testament and Hebrew. Since I am weak in the Old Testament, I have a better grasp of the New Testament and looking into the original language.

Pastor Monroe

It just so happen that in the major portion of my sermons, my mentor, Bishop A.T. Jones, taught us to read the major stories of the Bible and apply them to your life, e.g., Jesus and His parables, spiritual healing. I'm always looking at the stories in the life of Jesus; Jesus taking the little boy's lunch and feeding five thousand. If I leave the story in the historical context, it might not mean much to the people, but if I put it in today's context, Jesus is saying take what you have and give it to the Master, large or small. Put it in the Master's hands. He will add to it, multiply it, and subdivide it. What people fail to see is that even with a little bit, God can do what we can't do.

Pastor Horton

I see myself teaching more from the Old Testament and more from the Psalms than from the Gospels. But as a whole I try to preach the Old and the New Testaments.

Pastor Mann

Earlier you asked if there were any particular books that I preached for African Americans? No, I preach the whole Bible. Go back to Genesis when Joseph's brothers sold him into slavery. We see how things worked together for those who love God. Joseph loved God and we see what looked to be bad turned out to be good. So does the bad take away from the justice of God? I think not. God permitted that to happen in order to be magnified and to be glorified in the spiritual eyes of the people.

Pastor Boston

Earlier, I preached more from the New Testament, but recently I had a rude awaking to the Old Testament. I think I've moved to a 60/40 usage of the Old Testament and New Testament. The Old Testament now speaks to me move vividly than before.

12. To what extent is your preaching informed by the political and social issues of your congregation?

Pastor Table

Then here come the preacher and in spite of all you see, go and stand in the watchtower and wait. I try to come forth with messages with reality rather than superficial or perceived reality. God is the reality of truth, so I try to bring people along that avenue.

Olin's comments...I agree but I also believe it is also redemptive and renewing. The church is continually being renewed. New members are added. Those who come to faith in Christ are renewing. Like the skin, the church never changes, but is renewing. Like our skin, always the same but our skin changes every seven years. New skin makes it appear as though we are not losing skin, but we are losing the skin and it's being renewed, so the mystery of the renewing of the flesh is like the renewing of the church. People die and are replaced and the church is renewed. The church is strong although we appear weak; not just the church universal. After we came out of slavery they tried Jim Crow, which is a semi-slavery and segregation and tried to re-enslave us that way. So if the black church does not respond, there might be great suffering for our people and we should be responding more than we are now. I am not committed to the faith-based initiative response by the mayor or the president. I have some reservations and until they are settled, I may be still left out there because I believe the government wants a hold on the black church. If they get a hold on us for some money, then

Bush can dictate to me what I say on Sunday and my message is for Bush and the people, not Bush to the people. I'm not going to be a liaison to the people for Bush, but an ambassador to the people for God. So I must be able to say to the king, like when Elijah came to Ahab, I'm not the trouble of Israel. Elijah said, "No, I'm not the trouble, but you are. There shall not be dew or rain these three years." We have to say to Bush, "You will not be re-elected unless we say so." We must be able to command that kind of authority.

When I read about Samuel and people were afraid of Samuel because of his prayer life...I'm studying Samuel to understand the political, politics of that day. I see the church as the conscience of the state and I see the role for us as the salt of life, as aggressive on enemy territory. So we can't be passive, we must be aggressive with our message and stance. As a member of the black clergy, I got a call that we would endorse Alex Townage against Lynn Abraham for District Attorney, and I was in agreement. I was not agreeing on social and civic grounds, or political grounds. I was on the opposite side of the mayor whom I vowed to support. So I had to put a biblical spin on what I did. My conviction was that we needed justice in our city and for the records that were available to me. It was at a high cost for me, but I had to follow my feelings. Some white pastors are fearful of going against their congregation. That's fear!

Pastor Simms

I answered that in question eleven. I preach Babylon and get members to look at the news and see God in society, know what is happening on the political front. I want them to see how God is working things out. Don't be ignorant about world affairs, and especially about what God is doing in Israel and the rest of the world and the problems they're having with the Muslims. I'm very pro Israel. If you read the papers and see what is happening in Israel and the rest of the world, we should try to get our people to not be so narrow-minded, and not knowing what is going on in the rest of the world. So political and social issues, trying to get people to cut up their credit cards because if anything bad happens in this country, blacks are going to be affected more so. As if we don't have something in the inside to get along as in years passed. More blacks are committing suicide now than ever before. I think one reason is that we have gotten away from the Bible and Jesus Christ. So I'm aware of this and when I preach, I talk about it and everything in our sermons to keep our people informed and encouraged to read more, listen to the news and relate it to the Scriptures to see the hand of God and realize He is in charge. He has a plan and we are a part of that plan.

Liberation issues—some preachers don't want to preach about drinking, smoking, and other stuff. People won't like it if I talk about these evils. But I think that if we can straighten out my insides it will automatically do something on the outside.

Pastor Monroe

In a large church with about three thousand members, I am in constant contact with the mayor and the government. I encourage my people to read political information. But that is not my emphasis in my preaching. We are not involved heavily in our services because I feel that you have such a little chance to present the gospel to the congregation. I try to lift people to a different faith level, and economic level. We are sitting at the table now, two days after the tragedy in the United States. Yet, I sense God allows things to happen. This nation has strayed; maybe this is a wake-up call. We have a Supreme Court...I think this is the driving factor to the old land mark. So I am a great believer, that this is true.

Pastor Webb

When it comes down to politics, we have both religious and secular politics. So you are going to be involved in politics one way or the other, and some of us and our parishioners say we have no business in politics, but I believe that politics started with God's people, and I don't think it will be what it needs to be until God's people influence politics and put the right people in the right place. Our people have put us in a place that we don't have to answer to this world system and be caught up in this system. They can't say what they need to say so we must be their mouthpieces. The Old Testament teaches that the prophets went to the kings to pull his coat-tails when he got out of line. We still need to take that role and not allow the system to dictate what we do. So folks know where we stand and what we stand for. During the primary election for the mayor, I was the point person for the mayor. When I went down to get my assignment and an office was already for me, I told them that whatever I do, I will do it from my office instead of being downtown. It didn't set well with some folks, but I am a free man and did not allow them to tie up my time downtown.

Pastor Watson

It is what God wills for humankind. It is not political issues, but what God has to say about this particular matter. It is not so much as who to vote for, but try to see what side God is on for the people. If the issue is poverty, then God is on the side of the poor; if social justice, then God is on the side of those not treated justly. It is about putting it in reference to what God says and not my political opinion, in my preaching. Even outside of my preaching, I look at where God is. If a person at the University of Pennsylvania wants to buy up people's property, I'm not for the University of Pennsylvania. But I want to see to what extent those in power will use their power, and see if people are being disenfranchised. We need to do more than give our personal opinion, but see what side God is on. He is always for the downtrodden. Themes of importance in the black church have always been on liberation. The Hebrew boys in the fiery furnace, Daniel in the lions den, people of powerlessness and how God established them: the blind man, the crazy man having residence out in the cemetery, all were identified as the oppressed.

Pastor Hayes

God is moving and exists in all areas of life and much of what has happened in the Bible was politically moved. But I don't think that politics when it comes to the political world around us should come into the church and take over the church. But in the church, we have to deal with politics because it is a part of our lives, a part of our existence and even our justice. We have to vote as citizens of the United States and also as citizens and members of our congregations. So it plays a part as well in our secular world, but we can't allow it to take over our church. We must realize that we live in the world, but not of the world.

Pastor Mann

I do not use preaching to inform people of the political issues. However, there are times when issues need to be addressed. And I address those issues directly so that the pulpit is not used for political issues but that the pulpit is used for preaching and teaching God's Word. Yet, where those issues need a platform to be addressed, we help with that versus using the pulpit. I leave the pulpit for the Word of God. I'm very careful about mixing politics with preaching, but the social issues have to be addressed. Political issues need to be identified in a separate space.

The World Trade Center bombing issue, going to war, presidential approach—do I talk to the people about this? I think the political and social aspects come into the preaching under the heading of good and evil. I do not have a political issue for preaching. I put God as the head of whatever the circumstances are.

Pastor Boston

A part of the challenge of preaching is to help people see their need to be involved in the social and political issues in this society. We must be at the table when the economic pie is cut. I'd rather have some Christian folks there because then you know you will have someone to ask the right questions. And you will have someone there challenging how the slicing is done; someone to hold up rights for all of God's people rather than the slices going only to certain interest groups.

Pastor Horton

God is in and over the overall picture. My political view is I do not believe that we should get the church involved in politics. I believe in not having the voting booths in the church hall because there are plenty other places to have the voting booths other than in and on church property. I believe in a certain reverence for the church. When the Jewish people have their worship, do they have people up there dancing before their worship service? Why have Baptists started this dancing ministry before the regular worship services? Is that necessary to do in the church? How much of all this activity is biblically or religiously sound? The church is not perfect, but it is ridiculous what some of our churches are involved in.

Bibliography

Cone, H. James. *God of the Oppressed.* Minneapolis: The Seabury Press, 1975.

————*A Black Theology of Liberation: Twentieth Anniversary Edition.* Maryknoll: Orbis Books, 2001.

Dietrich, Bonhoeffer. *The Cost of Discipleship.* New York: Collier Books MacMillian Publishing Company, 1963.

Du Bois, W.E.B. *The Soul of Black Folks.* Millwood: Kraus-Thompson Organization Limited, 1973.

Evans, Jr., James H. *We Have Been Believers.* Minneapolis: Fortress Press, 1992.

Felder, Cain Hope, ed. *Stony the Road We Trod: African-American Interpretation.* Minneapolis: Fortress Press, 1991.

Harris, James H. *Liberation Preaching.* Minneapolis: Fortress Press, 1995.

Harvey, Van A. *A Handbook of Theological Terms*. New York: Collier Books MacMillan Publishing Company, 1964.

Hicks, Jr., H. Beecher. *My Soul's Been Anchored*. Grand Rapids: Zondervan Publishing House, 1998.

————*Preaching Through a Storm*. Grand Rapids: Zondervan Publishing House, 1987.

Hodgson, Peter C., and Robert H. King, eds. *Christian Theology: An Introduction to Its Traditions and Tasks*. Philadelphia: Fortress Press, 1985.

Hopkin, Dwight N. *Down, Up, and Over*. Minneapolis: Fortress Press, 2000.

Imasogie, Osadolor. "African Traditional Religion and the Christian Faith." *Review and Expositor*, Vol. 70 (Summer 1973).

LaRue, Cleophus J. *The Heart of Black Preaching*. Louisville: Westminister John Knox Press, 2000.

Lincoln, Eric C., and Mamiya H. Lawrence. *The Black Church in the African American Experience*. Durham and London: Duke University Press, 1990.

McClain, Willaim B. *Come Sunday: The Liturgy of Zion*. Nashville: Abingdon Press, 1990.

McMickle, Marvin A. *Preaching to the Black Middle Class.* Valley Forge: Judson Press, 2000.

Mitchell, Henry H. *Black Preaching.* New York: Harper & Row Publishers, 1970, 1979.

——*Black Preaching: The Recovery of a Powerful Art.* Nashville: Abingdon Press, 1990.

Moyd, Olin P. *The Sacred Art: Preaching and Theology in the African-American Tradition.* Valley Forge: Judson Press, 1995.

——*Redemption in Black Theology.* Valley Forge: Judson Press, 1979.

Proctor, D. Samuel. *How Shall They Hear? Effective Preaching For Vital Faith.* Valley Forge: Judson Press, 1992.

——*A Certain Sound of the Trumpet: Crafting a Sermon of Authority.* Valley Forge: Judson Press, 1992.

Raboteau, Albert J. *A Fire in the Bones: Reflection on African-American Religious History.* Boston: Beacon Press, 1995.

Roberts, Deotis J. *Africentric Christianity: A Theological Appraisal for Ministry.* Valley Forge: Judson Press, 2000.

————*Black Theology in Dialogue.* Philadelphia: The Westminister Press, 1987.

————*The Prophethood of Black Believers.* Louisville: Westminister John Knox Press, 1994.

Tisdale, Leonora Tubbs. *Preaching as Local Theology and Folk Art.* Minneapolis: Fortress Press, 1997.

Taylor, C. Gardner. *How Shall They Preach?* Elgin: Progressive Baptist Publishing House, 1977.